Shu

To Jack Adams,
the goodliest dean —

With WARM REGARDS
AND gRATITUDE.

Jim Shumaker
(alias Shu)

Nov. 1, 1989

Shu

Selected newspaper columns by Jim Shumaker
as published in *The Charlotte Observer*, 1974–1989

with drawings by Jeff MacNelly

Profile by Roland Giduz, publisher/collaborator

Dedicated to
**Doris Shumaker and Helen Giduz,
patient critics — and long-suffering spouses**

Published by Citizen Publishing
Box 44, Chapel Hill, NC 27514
Telephone: 919/942-2194

Library of Congress Catalog No. 89–85833
ISBN 0-9615867-1-0

About this book

Typesetting and layout by Universal Printing & Publishing, Chapel Hill, North Carolina
Printing and binding by Walsworth Publishing Company, Marceline, Missouri

CONTENTS

FOREWORD

My grandmother, like most rural residents of her day, had as one of the basic necessities a privy. It stood in various places on the downslope behind her house, leeward of the smokehouse and hogpen and chicken run. The privy was a two-holer with Sears & Roebuck and Montgomery Ward catalogs and newspapers for reading and conveniences.

The privy was situated over a hole in the ground, roughly three feet by five feet and six feet deep, unless the digger ran through Orange County's red clay and shale and hit granite; in that case the hole was shallower.

When the hole was nearly full, another would be dug and the privy moved. Then a good layer of lime would be cast into the old hole and the hole would be covered with topsoil.

My grandmother planted flowers on the old privy holes, as much to mark the danger zones as for beauty. Until the abandoned hole stabilized, with the topsoil settling and more being added periodically, an unwary soul could sink in there to his knees.

One of the worst times I had at old Granny's was in the middle of a December night when the trots suddenly hit me. I tore out of bed and out of the house and headed for the privy, ripping open my longjohns as I ran. Then I tripped and fell headlong into a hole from which the privy had just been moved.

That's roughly the way I got into writing newspaper columns; I fell into it in distress. I had been editor of *The Chapel Hill Newspaper* and its predecessor, *The Chapel Hill Weekly*, for 14 years when the publisher and I decided to part company, finally and irrevocably. He was tired of being surprised and embarrassed and often dismayed at what he read on the editorial page and I was tired of trying to make him understand that it was **my** newspaper, not his. So we turned away from each other without so much as a backward glance.

That left me in the awkward position of unemployed home mortgagee and sole provider for a wife and five ravenously hungry children.

To help me piece together a living — three of the pieces were piecework editorial writing, moderating a weekly television news program and teaching journalism part-time — Pete McKnight, editor of the *Charlotte Observer*, and Reese Cleghorn, editor of the editorial pages, suggested that I write a column. The only rules they laid down were to hold each column to 700 words or so and get it in on time.

For years the column appeared on Sunday on the editorial page. Then it was moved to the op-ed where it still appears. I figured the move was made so that no one could possibly confuse my stuff with the *Observer*'s editorial views.

All of the following pieces originally appeared in the *Observer* and their appearance herein is with the gracious consent of the present editor, Rich Oppel, and the editorial page editor, Ed Williams.

Neither Pete McKnight or Reese Cleghorn, now Dean of the College of Journalism at the University of Maryland, or Rich Oppel or Ed Williams should be held responsible for the contents. For that matter, neither should my old Granny.

Jim Shumaker
Caswell Beach, NC
July 30, 1989

by Doris Shumaker, 1977

PREFACE

"Shu" evolved accidentally. Jim Shumaker was a kindred spirit because we were both post-World War II veteran students at UNC-Chapel Hill. Our paths crossed slightly again as GI Bill graduate students at Columbia University in New York City. Soon after that string ran out we were back in Tar Heelia, both on the news staff of the *Durham Morning Herald*. Shu became state editor, while I left to become the first and only reporter for the *Chapel Hill Weekly*.

The appeal of hometown journalism was so great that when owner/editor Graves sold the *Weekly*, I joined with three other foolhardy and seasoned professionals to start up and publish a competing semi-weekly, *The Chapel Hill News Leader*. That audacious and controversial enterprise lasted five years. Meanwhile, Shu found an opportunity with the *Chapel Hill Weekly* (then become semi-weekly) and moved over to Chapel Hill as its managing editor, the same position he had at that time held in Durham.

Returning from a year's absence on a mass media fellowship at Harvard in 1959, I became editor of the weekly *News of Orange County* in Chapel Hill — in direct competition with Shu at the *Weekly*. Six years later that enterprise (*The News*) was sold — and to *The Weekly*. I found greener journalistic pastures with the UNC-Chapel Hill General Alumni Association. However, with Shu at the *Weekly* (soon to become the daily *Chapel Hill Newspaper*) I continued as a local columnist for many years. We communed and commiserated across his desk at our twice weekly meetings when I turned in my personal column to him as editor.

Shu followed me to the University campus, drifting gradually into full-time status on the journalism faculty. In 1982 I resigned from the Alumni Association to join The Village Companies at Chapel Hill in its various media enterprises. That necessarily and logically ended my columnist relationship with the competing *Chapel Hill Newspaper*.

For the glory and challenge of it all, I chose to publish a book about the columns I'd written over the previous 35 years. It was a self-satisfying product entitled *Who's Gonna Cover 'Em Up?* (The title is the punch-line of a traditional inside joke well-known to Chapel Hillians.) Shu graciously wrote a nice introduction to that tome. I asked him why he didn't do a book on his own columns. He said it was "too damn much work," which I knew to be absolutely true. In a never-regretted rash instant, I offered to write and publish it for him and he accepted.

As it turned out, that was only the beginning of our labors. I proposed and he agreed that his book, like mine, be based on excerpts from the personal columns he'd written for the editorial page of *The Charlotte Observer* during the previous 16 years. At my suggestion, he selected an arbitrarily agreed-upon 200 of those columns, and I went to work, organizing and writing a book, just as I'd done for my own columns. The completed manuscript was in 15 chapters on selected subjects. These were composed of direct and indirect quotes from his columns loosely tied together. Writing that took a couple of summers. Shu looked over the manuscript, and decided it would be better if written in the first instead of third person, as I'd done. On that basis we re-wrote it again.

— Was it the spirit of Thomas Wolfe, who allegedly valued as gold each word that he wrote? — Was it a legitimate judgment by Associate Professor of Journalism Shumaker on the quality of my writing and paraphrasing of his columns? — Or was it the precedent he found in published anthologies of other newspaper columnists? Whatever the reason, he decided the book would be better if the columns chosen for it were published pristine as originally written for *The Observer*. I agreed.

We selected 100 of his columns and grouped them in the six chapters of this book. The product, I believe, is exemplary of the crisp, articulate, and forthright style that has made Shu the best newspaper columnist in North Carolina — perhaps in the country today — in his free-wheeling very personal style. I am confident that you will enjoy this book immensely, and frequently empathize with Shu's trenchant writing and common touch.

It speaks to the spirit of those of us among the Great Unwashed who read the newspapers every day, but only occasionally come across something to which we can utter a heartfelt, "Amen, brother."

— Roland Giduz, publisher/collaborator
Summer 1989

ACKNOWLEDGEMENTS

This book has not been a simple creation, as was explained in the Preface. It has come to publication out of my conviction that Shu's writing and personal philosophy needed to be preserved in a more permanent format than the pages of the newspapers for which he continues to write.

Gratitude to present and future generations of people who enjoy excellence in prose is due my long-time good friend and colleague, Jim "Shu" Shumaker, whose skill and insight as a writer was well-known to many of us long before his latter-day comic strip model, "Shoe," was invented.

That creator, three-time Pulitzer Prize-winning syndicated artist Jeff MacNelly, has encouraged us in the publication of the book from its beginning. More important, he has generously permitted us to reprint some of his drawings appropriate to Shu himself, and he furthermore prepared and gave to us original drawings for the dust jacket and chapter heading pages.

The Charlotte Observer, its editors and especially its Librarian, Sara Klemmer, have graciously helped in every way requested of them.

We thank Becky Hollowell, a valued colleague at The Village Companies of Chapel Hill, for her enthusiasm and accuracy as she keyed in the text for this book.

Finally, as with my own earlier book, *Who's Gonna Cover 'Em Up?*, I thank Jim Heavner, President of The Village Companies of Chapel Hill, whose indulgence and mutual appreciation for Shu, has encouraged me in this venture.

— The publisher

PROFILE OF SHU

Praise doesn't truly please him in the fashion that anger does. When his writing excites praise, that is only what he expected. Anger, on the other hand, satisfies him as a reflection of what he himself felt. Shumaker likely wouldn't agree with (or give a damn about) this theory, but it suggests what motivates Shu as one of Tar Heelia's more dedicated and trenchant writers.

Though he is a tenured associate professor, a ghost editorial writer for two newspapers, and a long-time columnist, he disdains the glory, laud and honor that goes with any of these praiseworthy callings. Ask him for a description of himself, his philosophy of life, or his goals as a teacher and he'll likely answer in a few general monosyllabic words. I haven't interviewed him at all on any of these ideas. This sketch is written purely out of my own observations, with the added benefit of articles that several others have published previously.

Shu probably would admit to being a humble servant of the English language — a label penned by a colleague several years ago. At the same time, a simple, cutting observation he once made on his chosen profession is even more revealing. Asked by a student if he enjoyed writing, he answered incisively and simply: "No. But I enjoy having written."

His own writing on being a writer occasionally implies a self-deprecating feeling: You gain the impression that of all the facets of journalism he's pursued (and notwithstanding the many honors his readers and colleagues have thrust on him), he'd be quite content with a single-word description on his tombstone: "Newspaperman."

People outside that fraternity, of which he's been an active member for over 40 years, might think that a scant label for so versatile and capable a practitioner of the "craft," as he calls it. To Shu it says all that needs to be said.

From reading his columns, you will learn that he: (1) reveres and exemplifies the simple life; (2) has a scalding disdain for pomp, puffery, and pretense; and (3) relates completely to the foibles and natural vices of the common man. This is an incomplete chronicle, but a pretty representative cross-section.

It is also consistent with the visible Shumaker: totally casual, rumpled, lanky, in a semi-permanent slouch, and dressed approximately the same as when he was a GI veteran student in a lower quadrangle dormitory at UNC-Chapel Hill more than 40 years ago. A dalliance with the fashion of today is an ample moustache (presently shaved off), setting off his deeply tanned, heavily creased face and pale blue eyes. Shu found a necktie to wear (for the first time in years, he said) for the 1989 banquet at which he was inducted into the North Carolina Journalism Hall of Fame.

His statement of acceptance and thanks on that occasion gives a classically truthful portrait of the compleat Shu: "I thank the United States, which made it possible for me to attend this University on the GI Bill; the University for the honorary degree [actually, his earned AB] it awarded me 25 years later [in 1972]; the *Durham Morning Herald*, for teaching me how to get along on $24 a week; the Associated Press, for teaching me how to raise a family on $55 a week; the *Chapel Hill Weekly*, for teaching me the deeper meaning of the puritan work ethic; UNC Journalism School Dean Jack Adams, for rescuing me from unemployment; the present Dean, Richard Cole, for letting me pretend to be a professor; and finally, my wife and kids, for making it necessary for me to stay reasonably sober, and work several jobs at the same time...."

His students have several times chosen Shu as their favorite teacher. He no doubt quietly appreciated that honor, but it surely didn't go to his head. Typical of his opinion of today's student is this quote from a feature written on Shu in 1985: "They're bright as hell. They can get up on their feet and talk, and they're quick. But when they sit down and start trying to put one little word after another ... they can't write. They can't think. They have a very short attention span. Their minds are cluttered. They haven't read anything.

"With the students, the real motivation now is raw greed. There is unblushing materialism all over this country, and it would be unrealistic, I suppose, not to expect the students to reflect that."

The man who says all these cutting things has deep family roots in rural Orange County. He is the son of a hotel man (who gave Shu a middle name, Hampton, in token of his appreciation for the old Wade Hampton Hotel in Columbia, SC). Shu grew up in blue-collar Durham and finished high school there at a convenient time for Air Force service in World War II. His experience as a radio operator/gunner on a B-24 bomber came to an abrupt end during a 1944 mission over Albania when the plane was shot down and he was the only one in the crew of 10 to survive. He parachuted into enemy troops and spent the rest of the war in a German prisoner-of-war camp.

Shu's GI service entitled him to post-war studies at UNC-Chapel Hill. He didn't graduate then because he refused to take a required freshman course in hygiene. "Considering myself to be far too worldly, as well as a trifle elderly for a hygiene course, I gracefully declined," he explained. Hence, his explanation, as noted earlier, of the University awarding him an "honorary" degree 25 years later, when the hygiene requirement had been dropped.

He also attended Columbia University in New York City, courtesy of his veteran's entitlement. "Mainly, I took courses in drinking and playgoing and sometimes I even went to class," he recalls. "Eventually the GI Bill ran out, so I had to go to work."

Shu began his newspaper career as a city hall reporter for the *Durham Morning Herald* while a student at UNC-Chapel Hill. He later worked for the Associated Press in Charlotte and Columbia, SC — "the worst job I ever had," he later said. He worked his way through the hierarchy at the *Durham Morning Herald* to become managing editor there, and subsequently became managing editor and editor at the *Chapel Hill Weekly* for 15 years before finally joining the UNC journalism faculty.

During his Chapel Hill period he has left and returned five times and also had two wives and nine children. A combination of factors accounted for the repeated departures and returns to Chapel Hill. One of the earliest exits was inspired by the hygiene course case. His mercurial temperament, plus disagreements with *Weekly* publisher Orville Campbell, spurred another resignation to become editor of a paper on the Florida Gold Coast. He summarized that episode succinctly: "Two months later, after nearly suffocating in one of Florida's Cadillac cocoons, I was back in Chapel Hill, breathing the heady air of groves academe and listening to sophomores baying at the moon."

Another departure from Chapel Hill occurred in 1979 when he returned to one of his homes, Holden Beach, and became editorial page editor of *The Wilmington Star*. Reflecting on why he chose to leave the University community for what may not yet be a final time, he said "After Chapel Hill, a way of life almost anywhere else ought to seem fairly sensible — calm, orderly and at least semi-rational.

"Chapel Hill is standard small-town South only in population count. Jake

Wade, an accidental poet who wrote sports for *The Charlotte Observer*, once said in a line that will live forever ... 'Chapel Hill is a town touched by a strange magic.' Wade was about half right. Chapel Hill is, by ordinary standards, definitely touched. As a community it will rise up in full howl to save a single elm from the saw, a blighted and unsightly tree at that, and then sit silently, transfixed, while the Town Council flings good tax money at every vagrant wind that blows."

While Shu has lived in Caswell Beach on Oak Island for several years, he commutes to Chapel Hill for his Monday through Thursday journalism teaching duties. From time to time he still mutters about moving back to Chapel Hill, or some other Eden of the moment.

Shu's strongest journalism roots spring from student days at UNC-Chapel Hill under the casual inspiration of a latter-day soul-mate, Oscar J. "Skipper" Coffin. Skipper was a thoroughly un-academic chairman of what was then a four-member department of journalism. To understand Skipper is to better know Shu — who describes Skipper appreciatively as a "profane old reprobate."

Skipper generally disdained his campus office in favor of a table at the "Shack," a rough-hewn downtown beer joint which his wife ("Miss Gertrude") called "The Iron Lung — because Skipper can't breathe outside of it."

Of his own experience as a student in Skipper's editorial writing class, Shu remembers that "I didn't go to a single class. At the end of the quarter he called me into his office. He's sitting back behind the desk, wheezing and cussing, his china-blue eyes bulging out of his head, a cigar in his mouth. 'You owe me 10 editorials,' he said. The next morning I walked into his office with the 10 editorials tied in cotton twine. He glared at me and finally said, 'If I don't have to read them, you can have an A.' 'I'll take the A,' I said."

That was the end of Shu's editorial writing experience for a full decade until he joined *The Chapel Hill Weekly*. Since leaving it he's continued as a Sunday editorial page columnist for *The Charlotte Observer* and contributing editorial writer for *The Fayetteville Observer* and *The Wilmington Star*. His plain-spoken writing style reflects his own sometimes cynical, always skeptical, and usually humorous outlook on life. A Winston-Salem newspaper feature writer recently described Shu's writing as "irreverent and raw ... but his message is delivered with a twinkle in his eye...."

He claims to truly enjoy writing editorials. "You sit down and work off all your aggressions. I don't know how Moses felt when he was up there on Mount Sinai flinging down the tablets, but it must be roughly the same sensation." The Shu editorial sometimes reveals Moses-like anger. An example is the time he blasted the NC American Legion as "pigs at the trough" for supporting the controversial (and subsequently outlawed) speaker ban statute. Though that editorial caused the Legion to cancel its $50,000 a year newspaper printing contract with the *Chapel Hill Weekly*, publisher Orville Campbell never mentioned that fact to Shu.

His editorial brickbats cross ideologies, as when he called Sen. Jesse Helms and Gov. Jim Hunt "braying jackasses," and again when he referred to supporters of liberal US Sen. Gene McCarthy as "McCarthylings." A Shumaker editorial, according to tradition, can scorch the vanity of a politician at 100 paces.

Although his trenchant editorials won many awards for *The Weekly*, Shu became more of a celebrity when Pulitzer prize-winning editorial cartoonist Jeff MacNelly modeled the "Shoe" comic strip after Shumaker. MacNelly was a UNC student and part-time artist for the *Weekly* when Shu coached him on ideas for editorial cartoons.

From that experience, MacNelly later concocted P. Martin Shoemaker as the dour tennis-shoed, cigar-smoking bird who is a columnist for *The Treetops Tattler* in his "Shoe" comic strip. In his own opinion, Shu sees scant similarity between himself and P. Martin Shoemaker: "I have never in my life used a trash can for a desk. — orange crates, yes, trash cans, no." His own column written in reaction to that lionization is included in this book.

At his age of three-score and a half, Shu is a reluctant legend in his classroom. Despite open-heart surgery and a pacemaker installed two years ago, he disdains the notion of retiring before it's mandatory. "Hell, if it weren't for the honor of teaching, I'd probably go back to hustling pool."

— Roland Giduz
July 27, 1989

I
THE GROVES OF ACADEME

How students cope...

Class is just the place for zzzzzz

In another of those great leaps forward for Higher Education, a professor in Canada has discovered that students who party all night on weekends, carousing steadily from noon Friday until Monday morning without getting their proper nourishment and rest, lose practically all the higher learning they took on during the week.

A student can't go to a Friday afternoon beer bust, a Friday night dance, pull an all-nighter at a frat house, attend a Saturday morning brunch, a Saturday afternoon football game, a Saturday evening mixer, pull another all-nighter, run around all day Sunday nipping the hair of the dog, pull a third all-nighter in a row and expect to be at his or her best on Monday morning. Neither can the student, no matter how well-conditioned, expect higher learning to survive all those distractions.

The thing a student must do to learn all about man's march through the ages and retain it, and then to march himself or herself along the frontiers of knowledge, is to sit up straight in class, bright-eyed and alert, take copious notes, be respectful of the instructor, and then, brimming with knowledge, get some rest. That's what the professor found.

As a former student and as a practicing teacher, I can say with authority that the professor's findings are sound, if a bit understated.

In my student days at Chapel Hill, I went without proper nourishment and rest for an extended period, three and a half years, and forgot practically everything I learned. Toward the end I was in such bad shape that I forgot where most of my classes were. The University finally excused me from further attendance.

A good friend and classmate, whose name I won't mention out of kindness and sensitivity, even forgot where the University was and spent his sophomore year, on the GI Bill, running whiskey from Charlotte to Rutherford County, which was dry at the time and might still be for all I know.

He later made a modest fortune in Alaskan oil and hasn't had to hit a lick in years, but he says in all honesty that if he had it to do over again he would go to class and study and forgo bootlegging and get his rest, such is the attractiveness of higher learning.

As a teacher, with 8 o'clock classes every semester and in summer sessions (by choice — we elderly tend to rise early), I have seen students barely drag in, kind of feeling their way down the corridor, through the doorway, down the aisle, along the rows of desks. They then fall into place and sink back into a fitful sleep. Put a question to one and nudge him awake for an answer and the standard reply is "I'm sorry sir, I was thinking about something else."

A fellow teacher who retired early out of deep frustration had several strategies for keeping students awake. From time to time he would drop an unabridged dictionary flat on the floor with a terrible bang and then watch with a small smile as the students muttered in their sleep.

Sometimes he would stand at the back of the room and hurl erasers at the blackboard up front. (The University has an unwritten rule against professors hitting students, especially young women, with erasers.)

Now and then he would scrape his fingernails down the blackboard, setting up a terrible screech and sometimes bringing three or four students drowsily erect, working their faces and whining about all the noise.

I considered all these strategies to be beneath the dignity of the calling, of course, and refused to indulge in them. I tried instead to appeal to the students' sweet reason and cool logic.

At the first ding of the bell for an 8 o'clock class, I would lock the door and let all the late comers, which sometimes included about half the class, stand out there in the corridor hollering and whistling and stomping and banging, trying to get in. The commotion was nearly enough to wake the dead and just about right to get everybody in a good scholarly mood.
7/2/89

It wasn't character building...
Depression's mean legacy

In keeping with the times, the Ackland Museum here is exhibiting art from the 1930s, the years of the Great Depression.

One of the paintings is of a soup kitchen. Men in various attitudes of hopelessness and despair wait in line for their dippers of soup from a garbage can. The air is one of permanent defeat.

You might have heard that the Salvation Army is preparing to revive the soup kitchen program it ran during the Depression. Soup kitchens will possibly reappear by next spring, either regionally or nationally, depending on the need.

Another painting at the Ackland shows destitute men huddled together in a freight yard, preparing to slip aboard boxcars, a part of the vast army that shuttled back and forth across the country, riding the rails, in search of better times, better places, or just a job.

My late father-in-law, a tramp printer in his prime, spent several of the Depression years riding the main lines between Atlanta and Philadelphia. Occasionally he picked up a night's work as a sub at one of the metropolitan newspapers. I didn't understand how the family back home managed to survive, and he didn't say.

A home relief station, along with the soup kitchen a symbol of the Great Depression, is shown in an Ackland picture. The relief stations provided basic foodstuffs, mostly flour, for survival.

I used to go by the relief station set up at the old Pearl textile mill near my home in Durham. The men in that grim line would glance at me, a paperboy passing by, but they carefully avoided each other's eyes.

About half the subscribers on my paper route were textile workers. Through one stretch in the Depression when they were furloughed from work and broke, I had to decide between cutting them off or carrying them, a painful choice either way. I wound up carrying them, with timely loans from my father, and eventually collected most of the arrears.

The scenes in the Ackland, of a crowded employment agency, of men idling on a street corner, dime-a-dance girls entreating customers, and of tree plantings, were vivid reminders of those mean, hard years. The old Civilian Conservation Corps, in which unemployed, hungry and homeless young men found sanctuary, covered much of Western North Carolina with seedlings.

There should have been a picture in the exhibit of Durham's Christmas banquet for hungry children. The banquet was sponsored each year by a well-to-do tobacco man and held in the old Washington Duke Hotel. The newspaper always sent a reporter and photographer.

Now there was a rare juxtaposition of overweening pride, on the part of the tobacco man, and animal hunger finally sated, amid sumptuous surroundings – enough to fire the imagination of any artist.

About the only people pictured in the Ackland exhibit with any signs of spirit and hope were farm families. In a scene showing threshers at dinner, plates were piled high and everyone was filled with great vigor, in stark contrast to the Depression's standard victims.

A young lady standing beside me in front of a picture and, I suppose, noting my gray hair, asked if I remembered those years. The best answer probably would have been a tolerant chuckle and some homily about how the years of deprivation and suffering had improved the national character, strengthened our moral fiber and taught everybody the value of a dollar.

The Depression didn't do much of that, if any. Instead, it instilled bitterness, resentment, low-grade rage, and a sense of personal degradation and worthlessness that for many was overwhelming.

I didn't say that, of course. No point in spoiling anybody's holiday.
12/27/81

In no mood for Kidding...
Pass the food and drinks

I have been to some strange press conferences through the years, most of them as a reporter and a few in my role as a social critic.

One of the strangest was Kidd Brewer's going-in combination press conference-party several years ago in Raleigh. Kidd was getting ready to go to jail, as a result of doing some unusual business with the highway department and that was the occasion for the going-in press conference-party.

The thing took place at Kidd's palatial home overlooking a creekbed that is now Crabtree Valley Mall. Everybody stood around sipping drinks, not knowing whether to laugh or cry. The first question in the press conference part, from a reporter whose name I won't mention, was, "Well, Kidd, how does it feel to be going to jail?"

Another strange press conference was the one held at the P.O.E.T.S. Corner restaurant in Chapel Hill. This one was to announce the publication of a volume of poetry by John Myers who later became Chapel Hill's only practicing private detective.

John read some selections and the press conference eventually turned into what you might call a common drunk. A couple of reporters took notes but were unable to make them out later.

King Nyle, founder and first president of the Invisible University of

North Carolina, used to hold his press conferences in the West Franklin Street dairy bar in Chapel Hill, in a place called the Pit where students held debates and protest demonstrations, on street corners, anywhere he could collar a couple of reporters. Once, dressed in his full academic regalia, which I have never been able to describe adequately, King Nyle held a hastily called press conference at the foot off the Confederate statue on the UNC campus. There was no connection except that the statue provided an interesting backdrop in case anybody decided to take pictures.

A few years ago as a lark, not as a working reporter or in my role as social critic, I attended a UNC football press conference. The strange thing about this one was the aggressive behavior of the sports writers. They ate and drank everything in sight and kept hollering for more. As far as I could tell, that was the only reason for holding the press conference.

Bland Simpson held a press conference-party in Chapel Hill a few days ago and it was pretty much in this grand tradition. Bland is a musician, composer (*Diamond Studs* and *Hot Grog*), singer, and freelance writer. Mainly he is a free spirit.

His press conference was held in the Carolina Coffee Shop, which he also uses occasionally as an office. Bland and several members from the cast of *Diamond Studs* and six or seven reporters were at a table in back passing around beer from a cooler.

The reporters finished off the beer, ate the crackers from all the tables in the area, and finally worked around to asking Bland what he was up to. One of Bland's projects is an 8 mm film called *Zombie Love Bride*. Another is a nonfiction book based on an Eastern North Carolina murder.

A reporter said, "When are you guys going to do a musical based on the Joan Little trial?" and Bland said, "Right after we finish our Gary Gilmore musical."

The real reason for the press conference-party, it turned out, was to unveil a recording, music from *Diamond Studs*, and announce that *Hot Grog*, a musical based on Bluebeard's adventures, would open in Washington in March.

A reporter said indignantly, "Is that all you got us down here for?" Bland said no, and passed around free copies of the new recording. He also said that if anyone wanted to see *Hot Grog* at the Kennedy Center he would get them in free.

In keeping with the overall tone and indignity of the press conference-party, one side of the record wouldn't play.

1/30/77

Times have changed
Bus is a sign of prestige

The last time I rode a city bus with any regularity was back in the 1940s, before I made my pile, such as it is.

This was in Durham, which was pretty much a semi-roughneck tobacco and mill town at the time. I understand the town has taken on many municipal graces since then, but can't say for certain, not having been back lately.

Anyway, I was a good customer of the buses, dropping at least a couple of tokens a day into the Duke Power kitty. You could get three tokens for a quarter, thereby saving a nickel, and transfer tickets came free. I understand this has changed, too.

The bus clientele was made up almost exclusively of common laborers, department store clerks, bank tellers, domestics, those on the dole, bums, newspaper reporters, and others down on their luck. I was a newspaper reporter.

Once in a great while you might see one of the gentry climb aboard. This generally meant that his car was in the shop or had quit on the street, or he was drunk and didn't trust himself to drive. I heard that some of Durham's young well-to-do occasionally rode buses for a lark or on a dare. I can't say with absolute certainty.

Riding city buses in those days was considered a social stigma by many, a mark of humiliating defeat. I used to slip on and off as discreetly as possible, scrunching down in the seat when I was lucky enough to get one. In winter I turned up my coat collar and pulled down my hat and gazed steadily out the window with my head turned.

Well, I have taken to riding city buses again since moving back to Chapel Hill, and have found what you might call a transmogrification. Riding the bus is no longer a stigma; it has become a status symbol.

Men boarding buses in residential areas wear leisure suits or bush jackets and striped ties and all of them carry attache cases. The women look like the ones in Durham who would have crawled about on bleeding hands and knees rather than ride a bus.

It is all very warm and convivial, academics chatting about cosmic matters, the women about something the Junior League is up to. Not a single one seems to be ashamed to be there, riding a bus.

The only black I have ever seen on my bus is the driver. He sits up front, of course. The back of the bus, which was taken up by colored folks in the 1940s, is now taken up by professors grading papers and bankers comparing interest rates.

The other morning one of my neighbors joined me at our stop and while we were waiting for the bus his house cleaner arrived for work. She was driving an Olds 88. They nodded politely to one another, the master of the house and the cleaning woman. I almost had to smile.

Not only do the gentry ride buses now with consummate ease and grace, they take pride in it. At every opportunity they slip something into the conversation like "When I was riding the bus in this morning ..."

The ones who invite general opprobrium are those who drive cars everywhere, guzzling gas, polluting the atmosphere, congesting traffic, endangering pedestrians, and otherwise spoiling Chapel Hill's aesthetics. You mention going to lunch somewhere and the fellow who confesses, "Well, I've got my car," says it guiltily, blushing and cringing a little.

The transmogrification might be peculiar to Chapel Hill, this being a somewhat peculiar town. This is, for example, the only place I've lived where ragged clothes are for some reason badges of honor and people lunch on peanut butter sandwiches out of brown paper bags by choice.

The reason I started riding buses again, incidentally, had nothing to do with the social graces. My 1963 Dodge finally died.
9/19/76

Theatrical landmark lost...

The Varsity Theater is gone

Another Chapel Hill landmark of sorts has gone to dust, one of the few remaining reminders to those of us in our 50s of the way we were. The Varsity Theater on Franklin Street, in its prime as rowdy a movie house as a college student could ask, has been gutted and stripped to the bare brick.

Soon the hole left by the Varsity in the Franklin Street ambience will be filled by a theater specializing in art films, most of them, I suppose, with subtitles. Whether the change is for good or bad depends on your taste.

An art film house is being welcomed by some as a needed touch of class in the neighborhood, a sort of cultural bas-relief between Jeff's Confectionery (a newsstand/beer joint) and George's Cheep Joint (a head shop). Others who saw in the Varsity genuine character, if a trifle raunchy, are mourning.

The Varsity was, without halfway trying to be, in the finest college-town tradition. For one thing, it was hard to walk in the theater. Shoe soles tended to stick in the candy, popcorn, hamburger, hot dog, soft drink and beer spills. Occasionally patrons also would find themselves stuck to the seats.

University students made a practice of carrying on running dialogues with the actors on the screen, a conventional academic diversion. During a horror movie years ago a student shouted at the screen, "You scared the hell out of me," and stalked out of the theater.

Invariably, during moments of high drama and deep silence on the screen, a been can would hit the concrete floor and rattle down the incline.

Matinees at the Varsity, in sharp contrast to the evening shows, were downright restful. An advertising salesman for a newspaper I was connected with — a tired old fellow who needed his rest — napped soundly in the Varsity on weekday afternoons.

An old classmate of mine was the projectionist at the Varsity for a time. He had abandoned plans to become a doctor in favor of wandering from town to town.

On Sunday mornings he held free previews — Sam's Film Festival — for his friends and creditors. Delays between reels oftentimes stretched a film to three hours or so and once we watched a full reel upside-down.

Sam had similar projection problems during regular showings and toward the end was exchanging obscenities with the patrons, shouting down from the projection booth. At that point the management urged Sam to give up show business, and he switched to beach-combing.

In the mid-1960s the Varsity faced a crisis in its public relations. A woman claimed the theater had fleas and there was a terrible row. It's true, dogs wandered in and out. Now and then a bark or a whine would punctuate the students' running dialogues and some dogs bedded down there in foul weather. But, so far as I know, no one ever captured and identified beyond reasonable doubt a single flea.

In the late '60s or thereabouts the Varsity caught fire. While the fire department was drenching the place, the manager came loping out through the sheets of water clutching a box of tickets.

Renovated after the fire, the Varsity was soon returned to its standard condition, neo-shambles, and continued in its rich tradition. The *Rocky Horror Picture Show* was presented there at midnight for what seemed to be years and was still enjoying a good run when the end of the Varsity was announced.

That ought to give you a good idea of the staying power of fine art when it is presented in an appropriate setting to a sensitive audience.

10/3/82

Priorities in order...

Food for thought at UNC

Putting first things first and last things last, the university here has after 187 years gotten around to food. A well for drinking water, classroom buildings and dormitories came first, followed by students and professors, wagon and buggy service and other amenities.

Lately the university has been putting the finishing touches on high-rise parking decks, catwalks between buildings and media resource centers where you can get higher learning by videotape.

A couple of years ago the buildings and grounds department discovered an open space on the campus large enough for a volleyball game. A library complex about 10 stories high and who knows how many stories deep is now being completed thereon. The architecture is a mixture of Neo-Colonial and Modified McDonald's.

The university still doesn't have a monorail like Duke University's and there doesn't seem to be a plan for one. The considered Chapel Hill view is that Duke's monorail is academically tacky.

Now, following the natural order of things, the university has started wondering where in the world all those students are going to eat. Some thought also is being given to what might be served, and whether students ought to pay if they don't eat it.

The serious thinking in the upper reaches of the administration, as I understand it, is that soda pop and junk food machines are no longer adequate for a student body of more than 20,000. A steady diet of cheese crackers and Cokes contributes to student inertia and flatulence.

A committee has been studying the food problem for several years and is now on the verge of making a proposal. A part of the plan is to renovate a snack bar and improve a small underground feeding room that fell into disuse. In 1985, or thereabouts, the university might open a real dining hall.

A possible snag in the plan is the university's hesitation to get back into the food business, as one administration official put it.

In fact, the university never has been in the food business, although it has made half-hearted stabs at it.

During the Great Depression of the 1930s, the university operated a dining hall for students as an alternative to picking through garbage cans. Those who had tried both said the difference in the food quality was negligible.

In my student days following World War II, the main feeding station was Lenoir Hall. The standard exchange between student and counterman at Lenoir went something like this: "What's that?"

"What do you want?"

"Salisbury steak."

"That's Salisbury steak."

"It doesn't look like Salisbury steak."

"Well it is. Yesterday we called it beef liver. Today it's Salisbury steak. Tomorrow we're going to call it hamburger."

The University shut down Lenoir hurriedly and with finality after a riot there in 1969. The riot was not over food, which would have been understandable.

The turmoil broke out over whether dining hall workers should be classified as state employees or continue to be regarded as chattels. Liberals on the campus wanted them to be recognized as tenured faculty members.

Since the Lenoir embarrassment, the university has pretty much let non-athletes forge as best they can, not counting the soda pop and junk food.

That might account for much of the light-headedness in Chapel Hill — in case you've been wondering.

8/29/82

If only it could talk...

The bench with a past

The bench, which has served alternately as a social gathering place, doctor's office, and political campaign headquarters, is older than anybody still around can remember.

The clock, with "Coca-Cola 5 Cents" on the front, must be at least half a century old, the owner's wife figured.

The age of the scale, "Your Weight Free," is easy enough to fix. It is a 1925 model, the second set, bought new when the original wore out.

The old apothecary bottles were among the few things saved from the fire 10 or 12 years ago. The labels on the bottles were blistered by the heat and peeled off. The bottles are used now mostly for show, conversation pieces.

The apothecary bottles, the scales, the clock and the bench are about the last traces of Chapel Hill's last old-fashioned drug store. Next month the drug store will disappear.

Ben Courts is selling his stock, prescription list and presumably the drug store's good will, if that is transferable, to one of the discount drug chains. Ben will also join the chain. He is tired of trying to pay the rent which keeps going up and struggling to make it in a business where the personal touch no longer seems to matter.

To give you an idea of how old-fashioned the operation is, Courts still makes home deliveries. Ben calls customers by name and will open up in the middle of the night, on Sundays or holidays for someone in distress. That is as old-fashioned as antimacassars in the parlor or doctors making house calls. So of course the place must go.

The bench and the other holdovers from another age are from the old Eubanks Drug Store, predecessor of Courts Drugs. The bench sat in the front of Eubanks, giving a good wide-angle view of downtown Franklin Street.

Old Brack Lloyd, dead about 25 years now, used the bench as his doctor's office. He also had an office in his home but that was an auxiliary to the bench. They say the University built NC Memorial Hospital to take up the slack when Brack died.

Once Carl Durham was settled firmly in the Congress and didn't have to fret about opposition, he used the bench for his reelection campaign headquarters. Carl was a pharmacist in Eubanks when several Democratic elders conceded that he had more common sense than anybody else in the district and arranged for him to go to Washington. Carl occasionally used a rocking chair on his front porch for campaigning but that was only a concession to statesmanlike dignity. The bench in Eubanks was the main headquarters.

Clyde Eubanks, the proprietor, set the tone for the drug store. He was close with a dollar, instructing the clerks that, in case of fire while they were making a charge sale, they were first to enter the sale in the books and then call the fire department. At the same time, Chapel Hill housewives finding themselves short of cash at the end of the week, could tell their maids and cooks to go by Eubanks for their pay and have it put on their bills. Old man Eubanks willingly cooperated; I've never heard of Revco or Eckerds or Kerr handling that particular kind of trade.

Ben Courts carried on in the Eubanks tradition after the old man died, holding forth at the same location until the bank next door expanded and he was dispossessed. He was burned out of the next place down the street and took temporary quarters until moving to the present location, where the rent has become overwhelming. From place to place he took the old Eubanks tradition, as well as the bench, the scales, the clock and the antique apothecary jars.

I suppose every town that ever had an old-fashioned drug store has a story like this one to tell, or soon will have. The inexorable march of progress, if that's what it is, spares no one and nothing, and maybe there's no reason why it should. I still have trouble accepting it with good grace.
4/17/77

Dog Days now different...
Bygone Augusts in Chapel Hill

Those with hair white as the driven snow, or with hardly any at all, can remember when, in late August, you could stand in the middle of downtown Franklin Street and chunk a clod in any direction without fear of hitting anybody.

With the university students and most of the faculty members gone or in hiding, and those still about uniformly inert, the town had the urgency and haste of a turtle on a hot summer day.

The Franklin Street merchants, those who didn't have signs hanging on their doors saying "Gone Fishing" or "Tired — Back in September," lolled about, some lounging in their doorways gazing on the empty street, two or three gathering on the sidewalk to comment on the weather, and some dozing lightly in the backs of their stores, hauling themselves up and dragging to the cash register when somebody insisted on buying something.

You could park a car with ease practically anywhere, day or night. The sidewalk traffic was such that you could go hither and yon, lurching and weaving on a Saturday afternoon, as some beer-drinkers would do, without risk of bumping into anybody.

Louis Graves, the founder of the town's weekly newspaper, and his wife, both of whom moved slowly and carefully in their later years, and earlier and later tried to avoid crowds and hurly-burly, liked to grant audiences in late August. They would set up their folding chairs in the middle of the sidewalk on downtown Franklin, arrange themselves comfortably in a nice shady spot and then wait for the townspeople, those still in residence and ambulatory, to pay their respects.

When the world became too much with them, the Graveses would flee to Hillsborough, where the pace was even slower and the populace thinner than in Chapel Hill, and hide out, incommunicado, for a week or so in the Colonial Inn.

In my student days, when I lived in Chapel Hill year-round out of sore need and convenience, the liveliest place in the area and by far the loudest was a beer joint run by a bunch of GIs fresh out of service who still hadn't worked World War II completely out of their systems.

Even in late August the place throbbed daily, closed Sundays, from noon, when the owners tapped the first kegs, until about 2 a.m., when a sheriff's deputy would arrive with the noise complaints. The town limits hadn't reached the beer joint back then, and the sheriff's department had to listen to all the whining. The site of that old beer joint is now practically midtown.

About the only things moving on the university campus in late summer were squirrels, the resident dogs and an occasional young mother wheeling a baby across the hallowed sward.

You might see in the distance, in the shimmer of summer heat, a graybeard lugging an armload of books into the library and hear the Bell

Tower toll the hour, following it with a rendition of "How Dry I Am." But the place otherwise was dead as a doornail, limp as a rag and quiet as a tomb.

I was struck by the difference between then and now a couple of days ago when I came back to begin bracing myself for the new school year.

First off, I couldn't find a parking place. With the summer session ended, there didn't seem to be any reason for all those cars unless everybody was practicing for the September squeeze.

Then I had to stand in a long line at the supermarket checkout counter. The nouveau riche garage proprietor said he could work me in for a tune-up the day after tomorrow, and the barber shop that I used to stroll into any time of day and plop right into a chair now clips and shears only by appointment.

If I'd had the time and money, I would have checked into the Colonial Inn in Hillsborough for a little rest and rehabilitation.

8/21/88

An anachronism in the 'Southern Part'...

Struggle at the supermarket

The children, two of them, one about three-years-old and the other about five, had been giving her a hard time all the way through the supermarket, snatching things — candy and chewing gum, and cereal and cookies — off the shelves and loading them into the basket, then squalling when she gave them what-for and put the stuff back.

Exasperated when she had to replace a box of Little Debbies, she picked up the three-year-old and sat him down hard in the basket passenger seat and whispered fiercely in the 5-year-old's ear and slapped him half-heartedly on the rear. Then she looked around to see if anybody had noticed and, seeing me watching, smiled self-consciously.

She was wearing what we used to call flour-sack dresses when Pillsbury and the others sold flour in 100-pound bags patterned and with a wash-out brand name that could with a little needlework be turned into dresses and blouses or kerchiefs and sashes or curtains and pillowcases. Hers, like most of the old ones, was thin and shapeless and practically colorless from washing, a granny dress that some of today's college women wear for comfort, not out of need.

She had on a pair of men's brogans, better suited to plowing than genteel grocery shopping, with anklets turned down over the tops. The brogans looked as though she had done her share of plowing, or anyway, hard walking.

Her hair was straight as a stick and featured a pink ribbon tied in a bow on top of her head, her only concession to womanliness. She had tight sallow skin, the kind that sometimes comes from hard work but more often from a mean diet, and a lean, hard, angular body. She might have been 30 going on 50.

I followed along at a discreet distance, mainly to see what would happen next, watching her consulting a grocery list and closing her eyes from time to time, figuring.

At the meat counter she agonized long and hard, finally settling on a bone-in chuck roast, on special, fryer leg quarters, also on special, a pair of turkey drumsticks, a chunk of fatback and something that I couldn't make out without being downright obtrusive.

The children tuned up again at the dairy cases and she raced on past the ice cream before they could set up a really good howl. She picked up half a gallon of milk and then in another agonizing decision, studying the children briefly, took a quart of orange juice.

The checkout counters were crowded, and she bent over to look at the covers of the *National Enquirer* and *The Star* and one announcing that an 82-year-old woman had just delivered her 62nd baby, fathered by a 12-year-old, something like that, and slapped her children's hands when they went for the chewing gum and mints and then, finally relenting, tossed two candy bars into the basket. The children brightened up noticeably, and for one of the few times, shut up.

When her turn came at the cash register, she dug out a couple of discount coupons and watched intently as the clerk rang everything up and announced $52.20. She took a wad of bills from a change purse, counted the money and then began to take back.

Take back the chuck roast. Take back the orange juice. Take back this and that. The checkout clerk rolled her eyes, sighed heavily and ran the totals again. She was still 70 cents short. The clerk, hands on her hips, shook her head and waited impatiently in mild, nicely calculated disgust.

The woman touched the two candy bars and then, in an act that must have taken a lot out of her, said take back the turkey drumsticks. The clerk ran the total again, handed her the receipt and said paper bags or plastic.

She wheeled out of the store with the five-year-old hopping and skipping alongside, her head high, back straight, savoring a small victory of some kind — an anachronism if there ever was one here in the lush and affluent Southern Part of Heaven.

9/11/88

Arboreal atrocities recalled...
Better leaf those trees alone

This town has always been nutty about, in order of importance, trees, dogs and squirrels, along with talk, which is practically the only thing in Chapel Hill dirt-cheap.

The squirrels are not shot at, trapped or bedeviled, as they are in more conventional places. They roam the university campus in the heart of town, scampering alongside students and academics, secure in the knowledge that all is right in the squirrel world, not counting the confounded dogs.

The dogs, with a free run of the campus and comparatively free run of the town despite so-called legal restraints, occasionally chase the squirrels for exercise. But mainly they matriculate at the university, sleeping alongside students through classes and attending football games in Kenan Stadium, sometimes joining in the action on the field, and other outdoor events, especially those where edibles are served. They also attend commencement exercises each spring and have through the years strolled across the stage, to huge applause, while at least one U.S. president and several N.C. governors were speaking, separately, of course.

The trees are on a higher plane than those in most towns, standing in the sacramental order right after Thomas Wolfe, the Asheville novelist, and Choo-Choo Justice, the football player, also from Asheville, both of whose presence here as students became the stuff of legends.

At various times, depending on the level of nuttiness, which seems to go up and down with the humidity, or maybe it is the alignment of the planet or stock prices, Chapel Hill trees have been talked to, sung to (notably a Gregorian chant), embraced, danced with, and mourned deeply when cut.

The town was thrown into turmoil over the proposed felling of a ratty old diseased elm a few years ago. Public hearings were held to give distressed townspeople a chance to call down the wrath. The town finally felled the tree in the off-hours when no protesters were around to fling themselves upon the chainsaw.

A barbecue palace in a thoughtless moment felled a whole row of saplings to give passersby a clearer view of the place, infuriating tree-lovers all over town. Soon thereafter the barbecue palace, unable to draw flies, went out of business. New trees were planted and a seafood restaurant arose from the ashes, soon to flourish.

Tree horror stories abound here and are recalled in vivid detail each time another atrocity occurs, with those who have counted the limbs and leaves through the years shaking their gray old heads and clucking mournfully.

So it wasn't a surprise or considered at all untoward when the felling of two trees became a front-page news story last week, with a big black headline suitable for announcing a Bush or Dukakis political position.

The felling was by Duke Power Co., which has committed similar atrocities in the name of unfettered delivery of electricity. For years Duke Power had been topping the two trees to give power lines good clearance and then, with its sense of the proper order of things clearly blown, like a fuse, cut the trees down.

A homeowner accustomed to gazing on the trees with unutterable delight said in an impromptu lecture: "It's a big gaping hole that's opened up. I feel like I don't have any clothes on in my own own home," always a good possibility in the standard Chapel Hill household.

"At first I wanted to sue them for alienation of affection," the homeowner carried on. "I want Duke Power to be a responsible corporate citizen. If they're not going to do that then someone should rattle their cage."

Duke Power, in its turn, said it was unreasonable for everybody to expect the company to canvass the whole neighborhood every time it wanted to fell a tree to ensure the safe passage of electricity, and after all those years of trimming, it was time for the two trees to come down.

If it turns out later after deeper investigation that squirrels had been nesting in the two trees, or that dogs had been sniffing them regularly and lazing in their shade, Duke Power will really catch what-for, as it should.
9/25/88

For better or worse?...

Chapel Hill: retirement mecca?

This place, often touted as the Athens of Orange County, gateway to Carrboro, Beer-Drinking Capital of the Universe (a recent promotion from Beer-Drinking Capital of the World) and — the one that sets everybody's teeth on edge — the Southern Part of Heaven — has now been ranked as the finest town in the Sunbelt to retire to.

The ranking was in *Consumer Guide*'s "Best-Rated Retirement Cities & Towns," whose editors must have been out of their minds or maybe just out to play a cruel joke on the old folks.

The Chapel Hill-Carrboro Chamber of Commerce, dry washing its hands in eager anticipation, said the new ranking will increase immensely the number of old codgers coming to look over the town as a place to while away their golden years.

I have already investigated Chapel Hill as a final resting place and, as a public service, am happy to share my findings with anybody flaky enough to give the town a second thought as a retirement nest. I am a recognized authority on the matter, having moved to Chapel Hill six times in the last 43 years, the last five times with advanced anxiety. I recently said to my old lady in a light-headed moment: "Say, how about us retiring to Chapel Hill?" She said we can't afford to retire to nowhere, not even here in the house.

A good point, especially in reference to Chapel Hill, unless you happen to be Donald Trump or maybe Kenny Rogers, who just sold his place in Beverly Hills for $22.25 million.

The cost of land, houses and rentals in Chapel Hill or anywhere within easy commuting distance is fierce. A formerly unbuildable residential lot off Franklin Street, the main drag (which drags interminably now night and day), where people used to throw dead cats and empty six-packs, is being offered at $110,000. Unless the Rapture really does occur, a half-million dollar house soon will appear thereon.

A house that we built in 1960 for a grand total of $22,300 recently went for $114,000 and a country place that we had down in Chatham County, in the Chapel Hill outback, with an original cost of $33,500 for 10.5 acres, house and barn, is now valued at $190,000.

Rental property is not quite so dear, although it is also awesome. I have a sleep-in closet that converts into a living room capable of seating two, with kitchen and bath attached more or less as afterthoughts, and have had to take out only three bank loans so far this year.

Food costs, with due credit to the ingenuity of supermarket chains, are consistent with Chapel Hill housing costs. A package of chicken thighs that goes for 49 cents a pound in a supermarket in Brunswick County fetches $1.49 a pound in the same chain's Chapel Hill store. With the $1.49 a pound chicken thighs, of course, you get the Chapel Hill panache.

Eating out, which many old folks like to do, is in Chapel Hill an adventure in spending as well as in dining. A restaurant that trades heavily on its Southern charm will serve you a plate of grits for about $10, beverage extra. Meats and the like run into real money.

"Calabash-style" seafood also is available in the area and should be served with a deep blush, although it isn't. The real Calabash people down in Brunswick County would be startled at the prices and would hurt themselves laughing at the cooking.

To the town's credit, Chapel Hill is in several ways a good place to grow old, surely if not exactly gracefully. You can grow old in lines of traffic, in checkout lines at the grocery store, standing on the corner at Franklin and Columbia streets waiting for cars to let you cross, looking for a place to park, or waiting for the honor of having a standard Chapel Hill sales clerk take your money with a semi-snarl.

I have about decided to let the Chamber of Commerce quote from this piece in its next brochure for retirees if it asks in a really nice way.
9/18/88

To lose local landmark...

'Tin Can' to pass away

The University at Chapel Hill, which got flush financially during World War II and has been riding a hot streak ever since, is about to get shed of one of its last reminders of hard times.

The Tin Can, a metal barn that at one time or another has housed practically everything except cows, pretty soon will come tumbling down. The tumbling won't take much work; a stiff wind could almost do the job.

I went by there a few days ago on a sentimental journey, for a last look and maybe to recapture something of my lost youth. The trip seemed appropriate, my youth and the Tin Can being loosely intertwined.

The first time I entered the Tin Can was on a cold winter night in the late 1930s. I went to hear Jimmy Lunceford, whose band was among those pioneering swing, and discovered right off that it was necessary to dance to keep from freezing. There were steam pipes in there and they rattled to prove the heat was on, but oddly enough it seemed colder on the inside than out in the weather.

The steam heat, such as it was, amounted to a modernization. When the Tin Can was a new "temporary" structure in the 1920s, students had to rough it. At basketball games heaters were placed near the benches to keep the players semi-thawed. Spectators had to jump around and applaud vigorously to keep the circulation going.

The toilet facility was in keeping with the general ambience. There was only one. A male standing guard outside indicated when it was the men's toilet, a woman standing outside the door when it was the women's. They tried using a sign with "Men" lettered on one side and "Women" on the other but that didn't work because so many forgot to turn the sign the right way.

The Tin Can was also strange acoustically. At dances, in some areas you would begin wondering where the band had gone. Then you could move over a few steps and the music would almost tear your head off.

The Southern Conference indoor track meet used to be held there and it was a nice study in contrasts with officials dressed in tuxedos strolling about, runners drumming along the wood track, spectators melting in the oven-like heat, and a thin golden haze hanging over all.

Right after World War II, when veterans on the GI Bill were flooding into Chapel Hill, the Tin Can was transformed overnight into a dormitory. There was about an acre of double-deck bunks and risers and still the one toilet. I would have skipped higher learning rather than live there.

The last time I was in the Tin Can, up until a few days ago, was in the late 1940s, for a class picnic. The only thing I remember about the picnic is that it rained and the roof leaked.

Now, just inside the east door there is a sign announcing, "No jogging on indoor track. Reason — structure and age of track will not stand up under jogging conditions."

Nearly everything else was the same. There was still the smell of stale sweat. The roof still leaked. The steam pipes were still there, although no longer rattling. There was still the one toilet.

Cracked and yellowed photographs were tacked to a bulletin board on the south wall. One of the pictures showed Chunk Simmons, now a middle-aged Charlotte photographer, taking the hurdles.

The double doors on the north side were open, framing the modernistic concrete and glass student union across the street. The distance between the two buildings is only a few hundred feet. In other ways the buildings are a full generation apart. As the Preacher in Ecclesiastes said, one generation passeth away and another generation cometh.

6/27/76

The way it was back then...

Model-A holds memories

Three of us, the owner and a white-haired old gentleman and I, were standing in the shopping mall gazing upon a beautifully restored 1928 Model-A Ford roadster.

The owner said he had lavished about 2,000 hours in hard work and $3,500 in hard cash on the restoration. The Ford looked every minute and penny of it. You could see yourself in the deep luster of the fenders and body; the upholstery was precisely fitted and immaculate; the undercarriage looked as if it had just come off the assembly line and had never rattled down rutted roads. The roadster was authentic down to the last nut and bolt.

While we were standing there gazing upon it, a youngster came along dripping chocolate ice cream. He ran his hand along the fender, then stood on the runningboard for a look inside, hanging onto the window sill with his chocolaty hands.

The owner blanched, swallowed hard and hurried off somewhere to pull himself together. The youngster completed his inspection and strolled on down the mall, trailing chocolate ice cream.

The old gentleman smiled and said, "It takes you back doesn't it, these old cars?" I said I was just a child in 1928 even if I didn't look it now, but yes, I guess they did take you back.

He said he was retired now, living in Hillsborough, on the bank of the Mighty Eno, and driving his 17th Ford. In a very loose way, retirement to

Orange County and now this vintage auto show had brought him full circle, give or take two or three years.

He had first come to Orange County in 1923, to help build the Duke Power station at Eno. The weather at the time was cruel and he noticed that those working for Duke Power inside were a good deal more comfortable than the construction workers on the outside. So he asked the Duke Power superintendent for a job.

The superintendent asked him if he could handle all the office work and the payroll and help out with the boilers and generators and line work on the side. He said he could handle that all right. Anything would be better than working outside in that cold for 10 and 12 hours a day. That's how he began his career with Duke Power, at 20 cents an hour.

After several months, once he had caught onto the paper work and made himself generally indispensable, Duke Power raised his pay a nickel, to 25 cents an hour. That came to $13.50, for a 54-hour week and he could finally see where he was getting ahead.

In only three years he managed to save enough to buy his first Ford, a 1926 model costing 400 and some dollars, paying cash for it. Nobody would believe he had saved all that money out of the wages, but he had.

That first Ford played a big part in getting him married. Without it, his social contacts would have been limited to the Eno power plant and the boarding house at University Station where he took his meals, and neither one of those places offered much in the way of marriage possibilities. He chuckled and said, "In those days more marriage contracts were made in Fords than on the front porch, particularly the ones with rumble seats."

Later on, Duke Power transferred him and it wasn't until after retirement that he finally made it back to Orange County. He had promised his wife that they would come back some day, and although there had been times when he had his doubts, they had finally made it, four or five years ago.

The old boarding house where he took his meals is gone, along with the rest of University Station, and the power plant at Eno is fully automated now and there is seldom anyone around; there is no one around from the old days. But he can ride through those red clay hills and valleys in his 17th Ford and in his mind's eye see it the way it used to be.

We were still standing there gazing upon the 1928 Model-A when his wife came up and said she had been looking all over the place for him. It was time for lunch and she had heard that the cafeteria in the mall was very nice.

He gave me his name, but I've misplaced it. It doesn't matter. You know the type.

6/18/75

Carrboro's social center...

Summers at the ball field

In summer time the old ball field next to the Town Hall was the center of social and political intercourse in Carrboro, as well as the center of spirited softball play.

Teams sponsored by food stores, filling stations, laundry and dry cleaners, auto parts stores and other leading businesses competed nightly out there all summer long for the league championship and a chance for greater glory in district playoffs.

People started arriving early, at dusk before the lights went on, to claim their regular place on the grass around the infield and in the bleachers behind the backstop. The bleachers finally wore out and were removed out of consideration for life and limb.

Then milk crates, the old wooden ones in use before plastic crates and cardboard cartons came into vogue, began showing up behind the backstop, courtesy, I supposed, of the dairy that sponsored one of the teams.

Many fans brought their own accommodations — canvas chairs, stools, blankets and pillows, and a few, while the bleachers were still there, Carolina Blue stadium seats, the kind without legs that you just plop down on the boards.

Some of them brought supper along, fried chicken and barbecue sandwiches and hot dogs and thermoses of iced tea and lemonade. Picnic on the grounds with the sweet scent of mosquito repellent wafting across the spread.

The screaming and hollering, once play was under way, carried through the heart of town and sometimes, when the wind was right, out into the Carrboro suburb where we lived for five years.

At times the action in the bleachers and along the greensward was as spirited as the play on the field. I saw good friends fall out over a questionable call by the umpire and casual acquaintances come practically to blows over a close play at the plate.

The Mayor of Carrboro at the time, a portly and jolly fellow who liked to orate whenever as many as three people got together, represented the political element at the games, working the crowd with the same unctuousness that he spread at official functions. He was one of the few I've seen who gave the impression of carrying the weight of the world on his shoulders and at the same time enjoying it immensely.

The Mayor's great enthusiasm for softball, or anyway softball gatherings, carried over into regular town board meetings. When a particularly ear-splitting hue and cry went up from the ball field, those in the board meeting room in the Town Hall next door rushed to the open windows to see what was going on, the Mayor hot-footing it as fast as his bulk would allow, and the Town's official business died down.

I thought the softball breaks gave the Town Board meetings a nice touch, ranking in old-fashioned charm right after the Mayor's invocation in which he called on the Almighty to help Carrboro's sick and lame and halt, often mentioning the afflicted by name, and the intermission midway the meetings when everybody gathered around the soda pop machine in the corridor and the Mayor passed around sticks of gum to oil the oratory.

Each fall the outfield was used for Little League football and then in spring the diamond was returned to service for Little League and Pony League baseball.

But summer softball was far and away the main event, the year's sine qua non, as the academics say.

Now, in a burst of urban renewal of sorts, Carrboro is about to obliterate the old ball field in favor of a downtown park, with maybe a farmers' market, a bandstand gazebo, and a place for the yuppies' children to gambol.

Is absolutely nothing sacred anymore?

11/8/87

Van Gogh had a point...

Trying to quiet Chapel Hill

This animated wind tunnel, Chapel Hill, where talk is the most important product, ranging day and night from nicely modulated lectures to fraternity brothers baying at the moon, once again is undertaking a task comparable to cleaning out the Augean stables.

The Town Council, whose members are forever chattering away about one thing or another, their oratory at times gusting to gale force, wants everybody to knock off the confounded noise. The old gray Mayor, Jimmy Wallace, once again is leading the charge to hold down the racket.

The Mayor has made a public service career of sorts crusading against untoward commotion and in favor civility and gentility.

In his first inaugural address he hit a solid lick for golden silence, warning the Council members to refrain from uttering garbagnious rhetoric. The latest crusade is fully in keeping with that ringing inaugural remonstrance, although it is not aimed this time at Council members with a tendency to blow off.

The Council members are now out to bite the hands that feed them, in a sense, trying to gag, or at least muffle, fraternity members as well as culturally disadvantaged students and other rowdies. The Council wants everybody to stop yelling and screaming, screeching and harmonizing at full blast and otherwise disturbing the peace, by midnight or thereabouts, instead of carrying on all night long.

Besides the earlier deadline for hooting and hollering, the council wants to lower the legal decibel level. Under the old rules the maximum was 85 decibels; the new rule lowers it to 75. A vacuum cleaner inside a house throws 70 decibels a good 10 feet, for crying out loud.

To give you an idea of the Draconian nature of the new noise ordinance, two distinguished professors at the University here have just concluded a study of high school cheerleaders. They found that the average shout from a cheerleader in good voice was 101 decibels, or enough to carry nicely on a New York subway platform during rush hour. The professors also revealed another interesting finding, that people cheering alone, as some do, hollered eight percent louder than those who thought they were cheering as a group.

For all I know, the study will appear later in the *New England Journal of*

Medicine, as a warning to those worried about becoming hearing-impaired.

Chapel Hill's elderly, other than the Mayor, also are pulling mightily for a little quiet time. A Council member who has been in office long enough to be designated a historical landmark, pointed out that old folks need their sleep. Some aren't worth a durn unless they get six to eight hours, not counting naps.

The councilman figured that midnight was a good hour to call bedtime. That suggestion threw several bar owners into deep shock. One of them said, shoot, his customers didn't even get warmed up until around 10:30 and by midnight were just beginning to get into the real tumult and shouting. When I was a legal resident of Chapel Hill, living about four miles from the center of the action and measuring the noise waves washing over our house, I found that on weekends the crescendo came at roughly 2:30 a.m.

I haven't made an issue of it, but the noise was the main reason we got out of town, moving to Caswell Beach, which is about as far as you can get from Chapel Hill and still stay in the state. In one of those gentle ironies that some find amusing, the UNC students now come to the coast during holidays, spring and fall breaks and all summer long, and rival hurricanes in all-around noise.

Sometimes I think Van Gogh, who, you recall, cut off one of his ears, had a point.

2/15/87

Alma mater's Eden...

Arboretum: rest, study, romance

The place is a comparatively idyllic setting in the original campus, in what is now practically the heart of town, about as far as you can get from the madding crowd these days and still be in bounds.

The formal name is the Coker Arboretum, in memory of William C. Coker (1872-1953), the botany professor who preserved the little plot and filled it with plantings.

The Arboretum is circumscribed by a stone wall a couple of feet high and cross-hatched with gravel paths and brick walkways.

Besides the memorial to Coker and an outdoor botany classroom, the Arboretum is there, officially so designated, "for the enjoyment and education of all generations of University students." And they have indeed enjoyed.

Along the paths and walkways are wooden benches where aspiring young poets and essayists and novelists and playwrights and composers consult their muses. Others, merely looking for a lovely place to sit and eat, lunch from brown paper bags.

In fair weather and foul, young couples use the benches to vow their undying love, plight their troth (informally), and fix fraternity pins. They stroll hand-in-hand along the gravel paths and brick walkways in the thrall of whatever it was that brought them together.

In the center of the Arboretum is a broad greensward, and on a fine summer day or in late spring or early autumn, students, couples interested only in each other and some with an apparent interest in textbooks — and occasionally street people interested only in sleep — sprawl on the grass, taking the sun, stroked by the scented breezes wafting through Prof. Coker's plantings.

On a huge magnolia, high up now and out of reach of everybody except maybe a basketball center, carved initials have grown with the tree and are barely legible, V-something + JS.

In my student days 40-some years ago, the Arboretum was used for a final exam in botany class. Students filed along the paths identifying numbered plants and trees.

The way it went, the class scholar was at the head of the line, flanked by two football linemen. The scholar murmured the proper identification, one of the football players yelled it out and everybody put it down. It turned out to be an outstanding class.

Even now, at those times when traffic is gridlocked in Chapel Hill and most of the people in town seem to be leaning on their horns and pedestrian traffic is pell-mell, it is possible to sit in the Arboretum and with only a little self-conning, imagine that you are in an Eden, of sorts, without the snake and the apple, of course.

Despite all those wonderful advantages, or maybe in a way because of them, the Arboretum has been declared off-limits after dark. Stone pillars and wrought-iron gates will be erected at each of the 10 entrances and the place will be padlocked when that evening sun goes down.

It will still be ridiculously easy to step over the stone wall and sit on the wooden benches and sprawl on the greensward and stroll the brick walkways and gravel paths and maybe even carve initials on a tree, dark or not. The penalty for such flouting of constituted authority is not clear.

The campus cops can't run people off unless they are clearly involved in something untoward, but a warning can be issued that the Arboretum is a dangerous place to be after dark. There is some substance to such a warning.

A young woman was killed by an attacker in the Arboretum, but that was 20 or 25 years ago and it happened in broad daylight and there were witnesses and any number of people heard the screams. There hasn't been an attack of any kind — none has been reported anyway — in the last year or so.

Still, in these mean times you can't be too careful — a thought that probably never occurred to Prof. Coker.

12/4/88

Too much municipal 'whining'...

Stop nagging the frats

It was bad enough — going against rich tradition and human nature and all that — when the Town of Chapel Hill started interfering with the University fraternities' social customs.

The Town said stop setting up bars in the yard, out there in plain view of good, proper, God-fearing townspeople. Stop blocking the public right-of-way.

Stop scaring women and small children. Stop building bonfires in the front yard. Stop sculpting obscene snow statues.

Knock off the outdoor nudity. Stop bringing farm animals onto the premises. No more dangling people from second- and third-story windows and rooftops, even in good clean fun.

Don't do this or that or the other. Nag, nag, nag.

Then the Town started whining about the noises the fraternities were making — not just the blood-curdling screams in the middle of the night, but all kinds of noises, including the genteel hum of football mixers and beer busts.

Town officials would get within a mile or so of a frat party to check the decibel level and when the arrow on the meter went clean over to the right they would call in the cops, if you can believe it. Then the cops would tell the fraternity to hold it down; otherwise the brothers would be charged with disturbing the peace. Talk about party-poopers.

Now comes another indignity, an ultimatum of sorts, positive proof that fraternities are being discriminated against and have become an oppressed minority.

The Town of Chapel Hill has started condemning fraternity houses. So far, the Town building inspector, a nitpicker if there ever was one, has peered into 23 fraternity houses and declared 10 of them more or less unfit for human habitation.

The building inspector complained about such minor matters as holes in roofs, broken windows, smashed walls and ceilings and broken smoke detectors. The way he was carrying on, it's a wonder he didn't whine also about shattered glass on the floor, missing hand rails along the staircases, doorways with just the hinges hanging there, smashed light bulbs (instead of turning them off in the conventional way, you just sort of pinched them out), and the hostages screaming in the basement.

Almost any reasonable soul would say this has gone far enough, too much is too much, and the Town is way out of line. If the Town government isn't clearly certifiable, it has gone at least halfway 'round the bend.

Everybody knows that fraternity houses are supposed to be disaster scenes, for crying out loud. Show me a fraternity house where everything is whole and in place, where good order and calm and quiet prevail, and I'll show you a fraternity all of whose members are under felony indictments. In the natural order of things and in the finest American tradition, fraternity houses, inside and outside, are throwaway items. When the carpet, for example, becomes totally unsightly even in the brothers' eyes and reeks to the point that not even the house dogs will use it any longer, it is simply thrown away.

The same goes for furniture. The dining room table collapses and is thrown away, replaced by boards and saw horses. When the springs bust through the couches and chairs, they are thrown out and everybody sits or lies on the floor, depending on the circumstances.

Windows break and cardboard is inserted against the winter cold. If the front porch caves in, everybody starts using the back door and side entrances. When the chimney crumbles and slate starts falling from the roof, everybody tries to get out of the way.

Then, when the house is on the brink of collapse and promises to become a pile of rubble, the brothers of yore, those who have gone on to fame and fortune, are implored to save the house, along with the fraternity's sacred honor.

Why can't the building inspector understand that?

12/6/87

Deja vu demonstration...
Echoes of 25 years ago

For those who were here and as much as semi-conscious 25 years ago, the commotion Monday was, for all its differences, still a case of deja vu.

The commotion began, as it used to a quarter-century ago, on downtown Franklin Street, on the steps of the old Post Office, now the home of Chapel Hill's District Court.

The demonstrators this time, about a hundred or so, were there for the Martin Luther King Celebration of Unity and Conscience, sponsored by the Orange County Rainbow Coalition. The firebrands this time were railing against what they perceived to be the "institutionalized racism" at the University across the street and housing costs in the area, obscene by any standards. "Hey, hey, ho, ho, high rent has got to go," went the chant.

Twenty-five years ago the demonstrators, in the hundreds then, were signifying for equal public accommodations — entree for blacks to lunch counters, restaurants, theaters, water fountains, beer joints, restrooms, hotels and motels and the big waiting room in the bus station and those other places where the color bar had always held fast.

In the old days three of the ringleaders encamped at the Post Office flagpole and fasted for a month or so, a few feet from where the demonstrators carried on last Monday. One of them, John Dunne, dead long before his time, had been a Morehead Scholar at the university until he was seized by his conscience and dropped out of school for full-time agitating. Another faster, Pat Cusick, was atoning in his way for his forebears, one of whom had won acclaim as an Alabama Klansman. The third faster, Quentin Baker, had been a student at N.C. Central in Durham until he found his natural calling, warming up crowds for civil rights demonstrations.

The three of them sat and lay out there at the flagpole night and day, noticeably wasting away, drawing catcalls and jeers from the redneck element, warm praise and concern from the pure in heart.

There was nothing nearly that dramatic last Monday. After the demonstrators finished giving what-for to the University's institutionalized racism and high rent, they swung into that fine old civil rights hymn, "We Shall Overcome," and began marching down Franklin Street where so many had marched before.

This time there were no police and deputies lining the route to keep the peace. The old bread truck, painted black and converted into a Black Maria, wasn't around to haul demonstrators to jail for blocking the public way.

This time, if the walk hadn't been down the middle of the street and "We Shall Overcome" given voice, they could have been an exceptionally large Sunday school class out for a stroll.

A few photographers came upon the scene, shot quickly and left, but there was no network TV this time. Only a few reporters instead of a platoon paced along with the marchers. The roofs and upper-story windows, crammed with spectators in the long-ago, were empty.

Monday's march wound up, fittingly enough, at the First Baptist Church, once a citadel of sorts for civil rights agitation. And there stood once again the Rev. J.R. Manley, the church pastor, blessing the cause as he had so many times before.

Some of the towering figures of the civil rights movement had rallied the faithful in that sanctuary — James Farmer, Floyd McKissick, Al Lowenstein, Ralph Abernathy and a Rev. Stallworth from Alabama, a tiny fellow whose first name escapes me but whose fire and brimstone I will never forget.

They used to wind up the rousements at the First Baptist by marching around the corner to a drug store, owned and operated by a diehard segregationist, for a good-night demonstration and "We Shall Overcome" sing-along.

Monday, after the last word had been spoken and the last note sung, the demonstration ended there in the church, not with a bang but a genteel hum. The ending fit right in with the times.

1/24/88

Color of the language there...

Why the sky is Carolina blue

A new book, *American Averages, Amazing Facts of Everyday Life*, says that the average college student today throws in a dirty word for every 11 clean ones uttered.

If that doesn't shock you beyond repair, consider this Amazing Fact of Everyday Life: The average American woman is just as foul-mouthed as the average American man, except she chooses different dirty words.

I happen to be an authority in this particular field and from my own empirical research I would have to say the book's findings on filthy language are basically sound.

The 1-to-11 ratio for college students might be a trifle low. My research shows a daily average, not counting Sundays, of one ear-burner for every nine words fit for polite company.

Although your average woman does indeed sound like a mule skinner, her dirty word count, by my reckoning, is slightly lower than the average man's. She seems equally foul-mouthed because few expect words that will peel paint off the wall to flow from a dainty mouth.

Otherwise, the book's findings on casual cussing appear to be right on the mark. Or, as the average college student would put it, "(Deleted) well right."

Here in Chapel Hill, where thousands of college students are allowed to roam freely and speak at will, the air is what you might call electric blue. Profanity comes tripping off the tongue and falling on the ear, harshly or lightly depending on your orientation, as routinely as leaves fall in autumn. Those unaccustomed to earthy language are advised to use earplugs or turn off hearing aids.

I try not to use it myself, but I have been exposed to rough language since I was six, when I entered the first grade. The neighborhood I grew up in was semi-barbarian.

At 18, I came under the influence of a truly inspired curser, a drill sergeant from Newark, NJ. He used profanities for commas and periods as well as for emphasis, and threw profanity into the middle of a word, as in "For-(deleted)-ward march." Everybody got the idea right off and stepped out smartly.

For years I hung around newspapers, where the spoken word is a sight coarser than the written. A city editor in my experience had as his standard greeting on the telephone, without knowing or caring who he was talking to, "What the (deleted) do you want?"

Even so, toughened as I have become to language that will curl hair, I still blanch at some of the common parlance among college students. After all the years of listening to the spoken equivalent of battery acid, it still unnerves me to walk into a classroom and hear a coed, the essence of loveliness in her Calvin Klein jeans and Topsiders, barely beyond child-hood, let go with a molten stream of profanity after maybe hitting the wrong typewriter key. The first dozen or so times that happened, I was reduced to fumbling confusion; now I just blush.

Once I tried to correct a Chapel Hill student with a tongue like an acetylene torch. "Young lady," I said gently, "that word is a verb, not a noun. There is no authority, in Webster's or anywhere else that I know of, for using (deleted) as a noun."

She looked at me with great interest as if I were the very last of an endangered species, and said, "What the (deleted) are you talking about?"

I put her ratio at 1-to-6.

10/19/80

Career plans moving right along...

Diploma helps reporter drop 're'

This afternoon several thousand seniors at the University here, capped and gowned and learned, will receive diplomas at commencement exer-cises, position themselves for family snapshots at the Old Well, smiling indulgently, and then quit the groves of academe for the real world.

It is always a rare experience, this spring ritual, for those who only stand and watch as well as for those who grab their diplomas and run. There is something deeply moving in seeing young people who have spent four years (or five or six) preparing themselves for full and productive lives cut loose at last to test their mettle. The graduating seniors' eyes glitter and their red corpuscles race in anticipation of matching their hard-won educa-tion against the challenge.

One in the line of march this afternoon will be Ben Cornelius of

Winston-Salem. He has spent four years at Chapel Hill preparing himself and will receive a degree in journalism. Besides his sound grounding in journalism education, he picked up invaluable experience as managing editor of *The Daily Tar Heel*, the student newspaper.

"My future is secure," he said. "I'm going to work for Amtrak, as a porter."

And has his university education prepared him for this fine opportunity?

"Yes, and I'm glad you asked that," he said. "Let me see now. In March I rode the Southern Crescent from Washington to New Orleans. That's why I missed all those classes. Before that, of course, I rode the Montrealer from Washington to Canada. That was the last run before they cut the dining car and club car — a historic train ride."

Besides making the Montrealer and Southern Crescent runs, Cornelius spent much of his last academic year on what possibly could be called vocational education. He learned to wear suspenders, which are favored by train porters and conductors over belts. He started secreting his money in a leather pouch with a metal clasp instead of carrying it around loose in his pocket, coins jingling.

He also worked on telling time by a pocket watch with a face cover, a standard affectation among trainmen, instead of using a wrist watch.

Cornelius figures he is well-prepared educationally, for his new career. "Check me out on this," he said.

He went over to the door, tapped on it politely and called out, "Montgomery in 15 minutes, sir." Then he went about halfway through the southern leg: Mobile, Pascagoula, Biloxi, Gulfport, Bay St. Louis, New Orleans.

I asked to hear a good orotund "Booooarrrd." Cornelius said, "Wait a minute now, you're getting into the conductor's job. I'm starting out as a porter. I'm just getting out of college, you know."

In addition to his vocational education studies with the suspenders, money pouch, pocket watch, tapping on doors and calling out stations, he has spent considerable time adjusting himself psychologically to wearing a white porter's jacket. "I probably wouldn't have been able to make the transition smoothly without that C in psychology," he explained.

And in what other numerous ways had his fine university education, at huge taxpayer expense, prepared him to face the world, I asked.

"Well," he said, "Amtrak wanted to see a college diploma."

For a porter's job?

"I expect to be transferred to the office in Washington later," he said.

"You've got to have a college degree for that."

A degree in journalism?

"Amtrak said it didn't matter what it was in. They just wanted to see a diploma. Any kind." He popped his suspenders and said, "This printer, I'm not saying who, offered to make one up for me. He's got one of his own in his office showing he graduated from Duke. Printed it himself. All I had to do was pick out a university and he would run off a diploma."

Cornelius paused to reflect. "I considered Harvard for a minute," he said, "and then I turned him down. There's no substitute, of course, for a good education."

Of course.

5/14/78

Classy name might help...

Where the snuff trade is slow

The news that dipping snuff is enjoying unprecedented popularity across the country is certainly welcome in North Carolina, where tobacco has seen troubled times; but it is still hard to believe.

In Chapel Hill, which claims to be always on the cutting edge of change, snuff is not doing at all well. A random market survey found many retail outlets that carry a full line of other tobacco products displaying only a tin or two of Copenhagen and Skoal, usually stuck far back on the shelf. Requests for Tube Rose or Railroad or Plowboy's Delight brought only blank stares. Some stores had no snuff of any kind.

At Jeff's Campus Confectionery, where tobacco, newspapers and beer move briskly, Jim Mousmoules, the proprietor, said, "Don't carry snuff, never have, never will. I get all kinds in here and everybody gets along, but I'd just as soon do without the snuff trade."

The only one I could find in town who dipped snuff with any regularity was Lawrence Campbell, a Franklin Street printshop proprietor, and he didn't dip for long. Lawrence had to give up cigarettes last July due to age and other infirmities and, not wanting to harm the tobacco industry, he turned to snuff.

"Rumney's English," he said. "Fine ground, very nice. The trouble was that it kept trickling down my throat. Set my stomach on fire — I mean on fire."

Unable to stomach snuff, he tried sniffing Rumney's. "It cleared up my sinuses in a second," he said. "Practically blew the top of my head off. The only thing I can compare it to is the white lightning we used to drink down in Robeson County."

"They had the white in a galvanized bucket and sold it for 50 cents a dipper. The effect of sniffing Rumney's was a lot like the jolt you got from a dipper of Robeson popskull."

Lawrence is now on Levi Garrett chewing tobacco. "They put molasses in it," he said, "and it doesn't burn like Rumney's did. I get a lot of shirt stains and they are hard to get out, but it's not as bad as burning my clothes with cigarettes."

I gave up dipping snuff myself, with my grandmother's help, at the age of five. She was a regular snuff dipper for most of her life, taking Tube Rose by the lidful in her lower lip and using a dogwood twig chewed up at one end for a brush. The twig was used to dip into the can from time to time to replenish the original load.

(With its new popularity, the etiquette of snuff-dipping has changed considerably. Walt Garrison, an authority, says the proper etiquette now is to take a pinch — he pronounces it panch, to rhyme with ranch — instead of dumping in a whole lidful.)

My grandmother savored her snuff with such relish that I had to try it and I did, lifting her Tube Rose from her apron pocket. That was half a century or so ago and I have never once yearned for snuff since.

In a way the failure of snuff to catch on in Chapel Hill is surprising. A few years ago the University students, ever thoughtful of the environment, voted to prohibit smoking in classrooms.

Several professors turned discreetly to chewing tobacco and discovered that a wad in the jaw was hard to talk around without spluttering, and that a lectern, while handy for notes, was not a good spittoon.

Snuff would have been the ideal solution, of course, a means of mollifying the students without at the same time aggravating the Legislature.

If an enterprising company would come out with a brand named something like Phi Beta Kappa or Intellectual Dust, there might still be a chance.
1/10/82

II
LIFE IN THE COUNTRY
(Chatham County)

For swimming pool 'buffs'...

The old house has a new look

The most striking thing about the place now is the fine swimming pool gleaming in the thin winter sunlight.

The edge of the pool nearly meets the front stoop of the house. From the roadside, a couple of hundred yards away, it appears that the old fellow could open the door, step out onto the stoop, take a deep breath and dive in.

A second well has been dug for the pool and that was a sensible move. The first well pumped only four or five gallons a minute on its best days. The children in the house used to tax that supply just by flushing commodes, not counting the taps they left running. A swimming pool would have been more than the original well could handle.

A filtration system also has been set up, taking something away, to my mind, from the symmetry of the front yard. As I saw it, a peach tree in the right corner, a purple plum in the left, and a persimmon in between, along with a couple of young maples in the middle-distance gave the yard a nice balance. That is gone now, with the filtration system crowding the near side. It can be said, with reason, that it is no longer my worry, although I share some of the responsibility for the pool.

I was a consultant in the undertaking, you might say. The old fellow who bought the place, a retired golf professional from California, telephoned me to ask about the septic tank lines. He didn't want his new swimming pool to get mixed up with them.

He had been the first golf coach at the University in Chapel Hill, sometime around the 1930s. He didn't say and I didn't ask, but I supposed that he had come back to spend the time he had left among the memories.

He also asked about the water runoff, subsoil and a granite seam that runs through the property. I provided expert counsel, of course.

The pool, he said, was to indulge a habit developed in California, swimming in the nude. There isn't another house within sight and front-yard nudity wouldn't create a social problem except maybe for those driving along the road. I figured the idea alone, though, nude swimming by a fellow in his seventies, would be enough to rattle the sensibilities of the regular residents of Lystra Church Community.

That was the only time I talked to the old fellow and I have never seen him, the real estate transaction having been handled by a go-between. But there are several things to be said in his favor and I will say them given the chance.

The barn looks to be dignified and sturdy, as it should, considering the way we built it. The split-rail fence is in good repair, another reasonable expectation in light of our construction.

Something can be said for the pastures if you go for the manicured look, which I never did. As I understand it, the old fellow planned to use the pastures for practicing his iron shots instead of cantering a semi-blind quarter horse named Sam.

I have to admit the car parked in the driveway gives the place tone. I used to park a 15-year-old Dodge, a battered pickup, and for a while, a falling-apart Gibson tractor there. Folks kept knocking on the door and asking what was for sale. The Gibson, in fact, was, and I finally unloaded it on a good neighbor.

I hadn't been back for a long while and this time, on the way home from a meeting in Chatham County, I had turned in, on impulse. And I sat there on the side of the road taking inventory, in a manner of speaking.

Dwelling on the irretrievable past is a bootless exercise, of course, concocted of pure sentiment, and few have much patience for it. I don't plan to go again anytime soon, unless maybe the next owner converts the swimming pool into a watering trough.

2/5/78

Hear that, Wagner!?...

Culture comes to Bear Creek

Bear Creek sits out in the Chatham County veldt, 20 miles or so west-southwest of Lystra Church Community, which is the cultural capital of this region.

Bear Creek rests out there like an ordinary pumpkin waiting for a fairy godmother to come along and turn it into a handsome coach. The wait is patient and uncomplaining and hope is no longer brimming, if it ever was. Too many years have passed without much of anything happening.

The centerpiece of Bear Creek is the Post Office, a white frame building by the railroad tracks. From a distance, the building looks to be one-room with storage space in back.

Fields' general store, although long vacant and falling down, used to share attention with the Post Office as Bear Creek's downtown. The store burned down a couple of weeks ago and there is no prospect for a replacement.

There is a storage warehouse for chicken feed alongside the railroad tracks at the other end of town from the Post Office. Except for that, the Post Office, the remains of Fields' general store, and four or five houses, Bear Creek is largely undeveloped and altogether without pretense.

Across the tracks, around the bend and down the grade, on Bear Creek's outskirts, is Chatham Central High School, one of those impressive complexes that began springing up with consolidation. You expect to run into something like that out there in the Chatham veldt in the same way that you expect to run into Jackie Onassis. A one-room schoolhouse with a potbellied stove would fit more naturally into the Bear Creek scene.

On this morning the full rich sound of Wagner's "Traver Sinfonic" was flowing from the high school auditorium. You expect as a matter of course to hear Wagner in the Lystra community, home of the Lystra Baptist Church Choir. But out there in the veldt, on the outskirts of Bear Creek, it brings you up short.

Inside the auditorium, a fine amphitheater with plush seats, the UNC Wind Ensemble wound up the Wagner with a grand flourish. Chatham Central's students, the sons and daughters of our oppressed dairymen, chicken ranchers, dirt farmers, millworkers and those who kind of piece together a living as best they can, broke into sustained applause.

Then the ensemble went into a Milhaud concerto, getting rapt attention and some more vigorous applause. The same thing happened with a suite of movements from Rossini.

After the ensemble retired from the stage the curtain went up and UNC's Jazz Laboratory Band came on with a complex, wildly progressive arrangement of "Spinning Wheel." The Jazz Lab Band with its simplest stuff is not exactly your standard Saturday night square dance group. John Harding, the director, came out of the Stan Kenton school, and the Jazz Lab Band's intricacies make even Kenton sound conventional. The students broke out of their rapture again with heavy applause.

On the "Baja Run Suite" I searched throughout for the general drift without getting it once. My personal fog closed in completely on "Here's That Rainy Day." And when the trombones and trumpets let go on "Don't

Ever Leave Me," I nearly left them on account of my sinus. Then I looked around and the feet were tapping, fingers snapping, heads bobbing, shoulders weaving, and Chatham's sons and daughters were wreathed in smiles, understanding smiles.

John Harding, wearing a heavily brocaded mod shirt, the kind seldom seen in downtown Bear Creek, stood there in front of his jazz band taking it all in. Being a sensitive musician who must at one time or another have touched off a dud as well as exhilaration, he had to be startled at the reception in addition to being vastly pleased.

That's the way it went for about an hour and you could feel the special connection that sometimes is made between audience and performers. They were one, for an hour anyway.

And that's how culture came to Bear Creek, not with a whimper but with the soar and sweep of Wagner and the brassy blare of modern jazz.
4/16/75

The Chicken Bridge controversy...
It's not exactly a bridge too far

Nobody has asked me to take a stand on the Chicken Bridge controversy in Chatham County, but as a former resident of the area I feel compelled to. I support both sides.

Chicken Bridge spans the mighty Haw River near the conjunction of northern Chatham, southern Alamance and southern Orange counties. The bridge got its name several years ago when a truck trying to cross over wrecked, scattering chickens all over creation.

The controversy was set off by the Air Force. Jet trainers from Shaw Air Force Base near Sumter, SC, have been using the bridge for a make-believe target. The jets come sweeping in over the rolling hills of Chatham at practically treetop level and the pilots put their cross-hairs on Chicken Bridge, pretending it is part of a major supply route.

The jets don't drop bombs on the bridge, of course, or strafe it with machine gun fire or rockets. People ply the bridge daily and using live ammunition on them wouldn't be fair. The only things most of them would have to shoot back with would be the rifles and shotguns on the racks across the back windows of their pickups.

While the passes the jets make aren't lethal, they do make a terrible racket. Mrs. Elaine Chioso, whose house is near the bridge, says it is like living in a combat zone. Part of the reason the Chiosos moved out there was to get some peace and quiet.

Mrs. Marty Doyle, who runs a store near the bridge, is helping circulate petitions. The protest will be sent to Rep. Ike Andrews in Washington.

The Congressman is bound to be torn. He has a history of successfully restraining the Air Force, having stopped Pope Air Force Base planes from buzzing another bridge, the one spanning the Mighty Haw at Bynum. At the same time, the Congressman is known to be fond of low-level flying; he has collected dozens of tickets for speeding along North Carolina highways.

I am torn myself. Several years ago I spent a week vacationing at Bogue Inlet. The original plan was to spend two weeks there.

Planes from the Cherry Point Marine Air Base decided to use the sound for night dive-bombing practice. The Marine pilots made believe that our cottage and the ones around us were a Vietnam hamlet giving aid and comfort to the Cong, or so it seemed.

Every night as soon as it got dark, the jets would come screaming in, wrecking the TV picture and waking the baby. I got to the point where I would run out the front door and shake my fist at them, hurling oaths up at the night sky. That didn't bother the Marine pilots noticeably, but it made me feel a whole lot better.

At the end of the first week, we fled to the serenity of downtown Myrtle Beach. I, of course, wrote my Congressman. He sent a note thanking me for my interest in government affairs.

Balancing off the trauma from being buzzed regularly is the incomparable joy of make-believe dive-bombing and strafing. This is what splits me equally on the sides of the Chicken Bridge controversy.

As an aviation cadet in World War II, flying out of Hicks Field near Fort Worth, TX, I used to dive-bomb Eagle Rock Lake. Seeing fishermen dive from their boats and the prop wash kicking up water was a rare experience.

Several of us liked to clear the highway between Fort Worth and Dallas of traffic, flying wingtip-to-wingtip three or four feet off the pavement. On the last pass we ever made, a bus pulled over to the side to let us by and 50 or 60 passengers were craning out the windows taking down our plane numbers.

That episode converted several aviation cadets into radio operators, gunners and fry cooks.

I hope the fledglings from Shaw who keep winging over the Chicken Bridge are luckier. Some luckier, but not too much.

9/25/77

Would Chatham County like one?...

Could N.C. stand two Chapel Hills?

The Department of Health, Education and Welfare has given $65,304 to the University here to help Chatham County residents improve their environment, calling into question once again the sanity of the federal government.

The idea, as I understand it, is to help Chatham be more like Chapel Hill. This is a goal the people in Chapel Hill think everybody ought to aspire to.

The School of Public Health at the University will take the money and approach Chatham as if it were sort of an emerging area, a small Third World country.

Chapel Hill has extended formal recognition and diplomatic relations are being wrought. An advance party from the legation has already been down in the Chatham bush looking for natives and tribal leaders to tell them the good news. I hope the advance party gets back all right. There are several out in the Chatham veldt who in this particular case would be happy to assume the role of Idi Amin.

Once a nodding acquaintance has been established, Chatham residents will be urged to repair their rotting front porch steps, patch their leaking roofs and fix shaky hand-railings. The theory here is that they can never be more like Chapel Hill so long as the rain is pouring in and they keep falling through the steps and hurting themselves.

After the steps, roofs and hand-railings are in good shape, the grant program will move into Phase Two — killing rats, and beautification. Phase Three, the most important, will be mainly a matter of telling the natives how to get hold of money, like federal grants. If everybody learns how to get a grant out of Washington, the project can be called a success; Chatham will have become remarkably similar to Chapel Hill.

With shallow roots in both camps, having lived for a time in Chatham and living after a fashion in Chapel Hill now, I figured I ought to do what I could to help. As I conceived of my role, I would be something of a President Carter in the Egyptian-Israeli negotiations.

So I went down to the Crown station on 15-501 in Chatham and announced to the assemblage, "The University sent me down here to find out if you ignorant rednecks are willing to pull yourselves up out of your own mire." The University hadn't sent me anywhere, of course; I threw that part in for tone and dignity.

The Meacham minding the counter said, "I heard the University was getting out of football and going into social work fulltime." This produced hearty guffaws and several foot stompings. A functionary out of the county agent's office in Pittsboro, a State College graduate, whinnied appreciatively.

I described the federal grant program in considerable detail, explaining to Meacham that he might be able to replace the Pepsi crate outside the front door with a real stoop.

"You mean free?" Meacham said, brightening noticeably.

I said I wasn't sure about that, most of the money in federal grant programs being eaten up by administrative overhead. But the mission from Chapel Hill might be available for consultation if he would agree to build a little stoop out there and had the materials available.

"They might consult with you on catching some of these rats around here, too," I said. "I notice the edge of your hoop cheese over there has been nibbled."

"That was a Chapel Hill professor came in here and sampled the cheese while I wasn't looking," Meacham said.

I told Meacham that if he played his cards right and kept quiet about being a halfway-millionaire the mission from Chapel Hill might also consult with him about putting on a new roof. "The aim," I said, "is to make you grits conscious of your environment and quit living like a bunch of hogs."

Meacham banged down his Pepsi bottle like a gavel and said, "You gonna buy anything or not?"

11/26/78

For tolerating kids...
Give teachers a raise

Candidates for governor of North Carolina made their promises to the school teachers last weekend in a campaign ritual that has now become as institutionalized as barbecue and oratory.

According to reports on the gathering, everybody was more or less in favor of giving teachers a pay raise but only one or two were willing to say where they planned to get the money. Not a single one said anything about raising taxes, possibly because these days that amounts to the same thing as saying you don't want to get elected.

As it happened, none of the candidates had attended the Christmas concert put on in Pittsboro earlier in the week by the Horton Middle School bands. If they had, they would have told the teachers they were going to give them pay raises even if they had to go out and steal.

To tell the truth, I was a little surprised that there weren't any candidates at the concert. By my count, there must have been 400 of voting age in the Horton gymnasium and many in the audience would as soon have shaken hands and listened to promises as just sit there. I know they would have.

They went ahead with the concert anyway, and as luck would have it I got there about an hour early.

To appreciate the acoustics of the Horton gym without being there, you have to be able to imagine yourself sitting inside a huge bass drum. Every sound bounces off the walls, the dome and the hardwood floor, is augmented somehow, and then hits your ear like somebody slapping you up beside the head with an open palm.

When the band members started coming in, I nearly sprang out of my chair. I had never heard such a racket in my life, and they hadn't even started playing yet.

They spent the next half hour or so rearranging all the metal chairs on the hardwood floor. As best I could make out, they were trying to get the musicians in some kind of order that made sense tonally. This takes considerable doing with a band, such as the Beginners, where you've got 20 clarinets, four flutes, six saxophones, three trombones, 15 trumpets, one French horn, and 10 drummers. I understand there is also one violin player, but she wouldn't come.

After they finally got all the chairs situated, they spent the next half hour or so tuning up. I tried pulling my hat down over my ears but the old lady made me take it off, claiming I was embarrassing the children.

While all this was going on, several young louts chased each other along the wooden bleachers on the sides of the gym, their pounding feet adding to the terrible racket. A few of them fell to fighting, all in good fun, and generally disturbed what peace there was.

At last the band director, one of the bravest men I've ever seen, took his place in front and got the Concert Band to playing "The Star Spangled Banner." The national anthem was probably the only thing that could have brought on any kind of calm.

Once they got into it, the concert itself was just fine. All in all, it was as good a concert as you're likely to hear in the Horton Middle School gym.

As soon as the last strains died, the place broke into another terrible uproar and I had to stand around for 15 minutes or so while our young fellow searched for his music stand. The principal, as brave a soul as the band director, gazed out upon the turmoil and said it was pretty much standard student conduct.

There is supposed to be another concert next spring. Any candidate who hasn't promised a good teacher pay raise and figured out where to get the money by then ought to be required to attend.
12/17/75

A fountain in the living room...
Building a dream house

A family up the road moved into a new house a couple of weeks ago, and that was an event of some magnitude.

For most, moving into a new house is hardly enough to make the heart tremble. It's simply a matter of picking out a new place, arranging the financing, scrounging the down payment, moving in and the fine tuning of living.

For the family up the road, the new house represented an Everest they had climbed, an ocean they had crossed, dog-paddling, a scintillating victory against heavy odds. The victory was indescribably sweet because they had built the house themselves.

I passed the place three or four times a day weekdays, twice on Sundays, and saw them building the house, slowly and painstakingly, over the course of about four years. The building was slow because the man could work at it only in the afternoons and on weekends and during vacations from his regular job. Besides that, he couldn't or wouldn't order lumber and nails and roofing and the like until the money to pay for them was in hand, and money was often scarcer than time.

It was a family affair all the way. The man did the bricklaying, the rough and finished carpentry, hung the sheetrock, laid the roof and flooring, and nearly everything else. The only things he jobbed out were the plumbing and wiring, well and septic tank, which were beyond his skill and tools.

The children handed him lumber and nails and shingles, whatever was needed at the moment, fetched tools and generally made themselves useful. His wife helped to steady things in place while he nailed, held the end of the chalk string, things like that, and provisioned the crew with food and drink. Later on she got to be able to drive a pretty good nail and saw in a straight line.

In season, they parked their pickup truck by the highway and sold produce from their garden to passersby. The woman or the teen-age girl handled that operation while the others built. I often stopped there for corn and cantaloupes as well as to offer advice and encouragement.

They finally got the house dried in a couple of years ago, and most of the work after that was on the inside. Passing by on the road, I couldn't see much going on, but I could tell from the pickup outside and the open front door that they were still at it.

Once I stopped to check on the progress and the man and his wife were faced-off in the living room, going at each other with considerable fury. I left quietly, saving my advice and encouragement for another day.

The last things to go up were the brick veneer and the pillars for the front porch roof. He had turned the pillars himself on a borrowed lathe in Carrboro and they gave the house just the right touch.

The family gave me the grand tour right after the house was finished, before they moved in and the landscaping was done, and it was then that I got the details of that furious argument in the middle of the living room.

"He wanted a fountain right smack in the middle of the living room," the wife said. "Can you feature that?"

"I always wanted a house with a fountain in the middle," he said. "You know, with the bedrooms on one end, the kitchen and dining room and family room on the other end, and right there in the middle a big fountain to sit around. I'm talking about a real fountain made out of stone, running water with lights playing on it, plants, everything." He looked at his wife and said, "What's so cockeyed about that?" The house was finished, a turnkey job, but his dream of a fountain clearly was not.

"I'll tell you what's cockeyed about it," she said. "The whole idea, that's what's cockeyed. Anybody that thinks I'm going to spend all my time mopping the living room floor and trying to keep children out of a fountain has got another thought coming." She looked at me and said, "Have you ever tried to arrange living room furniture around a fountain?" I hadn't, and for once failed to offer any advice and encouragement. I didn't say anything, but if somebody had held a gun to my head and told me to vote I would have gone for the fountain.

He looked around the living room with a certain regret and said, "Anybody can build a conventional house."

Sure they can.

7/20/75

Discord in the choir loft...

Joyful noises in Lystra

The Lystra Baptist Church adult and youth choirs are being combined this year for the Christmas program, and from what I have seen so far it is a terrible mistake.

Members of the choirs range in age from 10 to about 75. In keeping with the equal rights movement, males and females are about even — in number, not voice. I give the males an edge in vocal quality.

According to the plan, the sanctuary will be plunged into darkness for the program and the choir members, each carrying a lighted candle, will march double-file down the aisles. Then, if the church hasn't been set afire, they will gather on the dais and make joyful noise.

We got into trouble at the beginning of the first practice. The choir director, who as a rural letter carrier has no problem getting the mail into the right boxes all over the county, couldn't divide the members into two groups.

Everybody congregated in one aisle. The director said that wouldn't work, so everybody congregated in the other aisle. It took about 20 minutes for him to parcel us out into two bunches. If our choir director had been in Eisenhower's shoes planning the Normandy invasion, World War II would have ended a lot sooner. The Germans would have laughed themselves sick and the Allies could have walked right in.

As soon as the two bunches were formed and everybody got lined up, an 11-year-old boy announced that he wasn't about to march down no aisle with no woman. That's the way some 11-year-olds talk down here, some 50-year-olds, too. That problem was solved by pairing him with the preacher's wife, a stunning young woman.

The choir members made it down the aisles somehow, the young practically running and the elderly dragging along, singing "Hark, the Herald Angels Sing" as they went. The singing was ragged, but you have to remember that this was the first time in that particular formation.

The choir director got us strung out along the dais after a period of stumbling around and we went into our first number, beginning nearly together. I had never heard the thing before, anywhere, and I asked the director if we were going to put on a regular American Christmas program. He was getting a little testy by then and he said no, we were going to put on a Polish Christmas program.

Then someone suggested that it was going to be a trifle awkward holding a lighted candle in one hand and music in the other, singing and trying to turn pages all at once. The 11-year-old who had announced that he wasn't going to march down no aisle with no woman said he planned to turn the pages with his nose, and did it to show everybody that he could.

About midway through "Silent Night," one of my favorites, an alto in front turned around and asked what I was singing. I told her I had gone along with the melody on the first verse, tenor on the second, and was thinking about trying maybe a rich baritone or bass the rest of the way. She said that was all right but to try not to switch around in the middle of a note.

We went through the whole program, doggedly, and everybody could see that the choir director's brows were beginning to knit. I felt sorry for the poor fellow, so at the end I smiled brightly and said, "I don't think that sounded too bad." Everybody looked around to see who in the world had said it.

Personally, I would just as soon put on the same program we gave last year. I was a king from the Orient in that one. All I had to do was stand there draped in a bedspread and with a towel wrapped around my head. Several folks said I had gotten it down just about right.

12/10/75

Think again, pastor...

Misadventures in Scouting

I have here an envelope containing three pounds of material on the organization, care and feeding of a Boy Scout troop.

The envelope turned up in my mailbox, left there by one of the flock of Lystra Baptist Church, which, of course, is right here in the Lystra Church Community.

When I caught the pastor unawares, I told him I had looked over the material with great nostalgia and some interest, but was puzzled as to why it had been sent to me. The pastor bridled and finally got it out that I had been chosen to organize and lead a Boy Scout troop.

I asked him how this signal honor had fallen to me and he said, "Well, the other members of the congregation are already doing good constructive work. Besides, we understand you've had experience in scouting."

I admit that's true. I was present for the creation and dissolution of a scout troop in Durham back during the Great Depression. The troop was sponsored by Watts Street Baptist Church, and it was probably the most God-forsaken missionary work ever attempted. The deacons later conceded as much.

The troop met in the church basement and that's where the trouble began. It was one thing to try to lead a gang of ruffians into wholesome young manhood, but all that racket coming from a church just didn't seem right. Residents of the neighborhood started complaining.

The scoutmaster took to playing the accordion to calm us and setting up community sings to keep fellowship flowing. The neighbors couldn't decide which they hated most, yelling and screaming or accordion playing and singing. The scoutmaster hit on an inspiration and started sending us out of town on 14-mile hikes and camping trips.

It was on those 14-mile hikes that we took up drinking and smoking. In those days you could get a beer and a pack of Wings for a quarter. The patrol leader took up the money and he would go into the first general store handy for supplies. That went on until reports got back to town about Boy Scouts hiking along the highway swilling beer and trailing cigarette smoke.

The camping trips led as much as anything, I suppose, to dissolution of the troop. A civic-minded citizen let us use his acreage about 12 miles from town for camping, studying nature, and tying each other to trees. There was an abandoned tenant house in a broomstraw field, creek, piney woods, and not much else.

The trouble started when one of us decided to practice hatchet-throwing. A nice pine was selected and the hatchet-throwing proceeded. After the bark was pretty well peeled off that one, another pine was selected, and then another, and another. When the scoutmaster came upon thosed skinned pines he blanched, sucked in his breath, and stood there working his lips.

We probably could have gotten away with the tree surgery if it hadn't been for the fire. Spero Dorton, whose father owned a restaurant, had brought along a steak to help tide him over the weekend. He was trying to cook it in the broomstraw field and got careless with his cigarette lighter. There was a nice breeze and the field just went whoosh, the way he told it.

Spero took off running for the tenant house to put his steak in a safe place and I took off running to spread the alarm.

By the time I got back, the broomstraw field was cleared, everything neatly charred except the tenant house. The others, bored with fighting fire, were whooping it up down at the creek.

When the scoutmaster came out from town after work, he didn't say much of anything for the longest kind of time. His lips worked, like they had when he saw the skinned pines, and his eyes misted over, but mostly he just walked around the charred field shaking his head.

A couple of weeks later the troop was dissolved, "for the good of every-one concerned," which took in a lot of folks counting all those living around Watts Street Baptist Church.

I haven't been back to Lystra Baptist since the parson explained what the Boy Scout material was for, and don't plan to return until the flock gets dead set on some other kind of project.

9/29/74

So long, Chatham County...
We will just drive away

How do you say goodbye to a farm that yielded practically nothing but pleasure?

I suppose I could go out and sit on the granite outcropping beside the giant cedar, just beyond the well house, and watch the sun sink slowly beneath the line of pines to the west. Sitting there, looking back down the years, it ought to be easy enough to work up a melancholy mood, a lump in the throat and a little mist in the eyes.

The trouble is that it's a sweltering 90 degrees out there now. Wasps have nested inside the well house and it would be touch-and-go trying to sustain a melancholy mood while fighting off wasps and dripping sweat.

I could stroll around the property one last time, I suppose, fingering the electric fence that seldom worked, surveying the pasture so hard-won, and seeing how the persimmons were coming along. I could linger among the trees counting the fireplace wood, cut and still ungathered, and pause to chunk one more rock into the creek on the backside.

The electric fence is rusting now and down in some places. I let it go after we sold off the horses. The stalls on the lee side of the barn have fallen into disrepair, too, and are now filled mostly with junk, the detritus of a life in the country that is ending.

The pasture is overgrown now and choked with weeds and would make for rough strolling. I have let the pasture go, too, since the agreement to sell was signed.

The persimmon crop figures to be heavy, one that I would like to see fall. I don't know who will be gathering the persimmons, or the firewood, cut to length and just lying there among the trees, or whether anyone will. Not that it will be my concern any longer.

The most appropriate place to say goodbye, maybe, would be at the barn, my over-arching pride, first, last and always. I built it, with a little help from my friends, and it is sounder architecturally and more satisfying aesthetically than the house, which was built by a licensed contractor.

My friends and I also built the well house; I rank it behind the barn but still ahead of the contractor's work.

The barn now is a crazy litter of magazines, newspapers, paperback books, canceled checks, letters falling to pieces with age, and Christmas cards I neglected to send. Rats have been at the canceled checks but that is no great loss.

Somewhere in the litter is part of a novel, begun 25 years ago and finally abandoned with great relief. The discard pile is a fit place for the novel to come to its final rest, and I didn't need a publisher to tell me.

Once, in an excess of ambition and confidence, I planned to become the home brew king of Chatham County. I spent days collecting Budweiser bottles, the old-fashioned tall brown ones, a dozen or so cases, and put in a complete brewing outfit. The crock and bottles are still over in a corner of the barn collecting dust and cobwebs. The capper and hydrometer and tubes and other paraphernalia disappeared long ago. In its present condition, wild disarray, the barn is no place for sentimentalizing.

I guess I could go out and sit on the split-rail cedar fence along the drive and spit in the dust and think about leaving. There must be a good thousand feet of the fence and it is safe to sit on. I know, because I put it up, dug every posthole myself, by hand, and sighted and fit every rail, without any help from my friends. They got cured on the barn and well house.

And then, instead of saying goodbye to the farm, I could just say the hell with it and get in the car and drive away. That's what I plan to do.
7/14/76

A fortune in junk...
That was some yard sale!

I took time off between worrying about detente and concocting stories for the Internal Revenue, to attend the Lystra Baptist Church yard sale. My word is generally good enough, but you had to see this one to believe it.

I have seldom seen so many strange items gathered together for sale in one place. The only thing to rival it in my experience was the E.A. Brown new and used furniture store in Chapel Hill.

Old man Brown was close to 90 when he went to his reward. Practically up to the time of his departure he tended the furniture store and observed human folly in Chapel Hill. Anyone observing human folly in Chapel Hill can make it a full-time job if he wants to.

I'm sure he saw order and symmetry in his inventory, even though everybody else said it was a mess. You could go in there and ask for something and he would say, "Look around; there might be one in here someplace. If you can't find it maybe you'll settle on something else."

I went in Brown's once with the notion that I needed a roll-top desk to go with my views on life. He had one and was willing to part with it.

The price was too much for me to handle, but I got into the spirit of the place and bought a wash basin and pitcher and a tintype of an elderly couple, total strangers, made around the turn of the century.

I never could figure out why I bought the wash basin and pitcher. The only explanation I could give for the tintype was that it reminded me of Grant Wood's *American Gothic*.

Some said old man Brown went into decline once he realized that Orange County, led by Chapel Hill, had become permanently Democratic. I figured his decline was on account of cars. One bowled him over in Chapel Hill. Then another one tore into the side of his furniture store, caving in one wall and messing up his inventory. Brown was the only one who could tell anything was out of place.

I got to Brown's right after the car had entered through the east wall. All agreed it was a terrible thing to happen to anybody, even a practicing Republican.

Lystra Baptist's yard sale reminded me right off of Brown's furniture store after the crash. You couldn't tell whether some of the things were there by design or had been blown in by the wind. Except for the pony, of course. The first time I noticed the pony it was tethered on the lawn and seemed contented enough. The next time I noticed, the pony was galloping down the Pittsboro highway with half the congregation giving chase. The pony brought $10 and the Lystra flock was relieved at the sale.

Our contribution was two lamps made out of genuine wagon wheel hubs, each weighing about 50 pounds, and an original oil painting. I nearly ruined my back getting the lamps out of the barn where they had qualified over the years as antiques. (I plan to put down the oil painting as a charitable contribution worth $1,500. It will give the Internal Revenue auditor a good laugh and maybe brighten his spirits.)

After the yard sale wound up and we were standing around saying how much good we had done for the church, I told one of the deacons how glad I was to be able to finally unload those lamps. I carried on for two or three minutes about how awful they were, barely fit for a bonfire, before I noticed his discomfort.

It turned out the deacon's wife had bought the lamps and was getting ready to make them conversation pieces of some kind. She paid twice as much as the pony brought, which might say something about today's economy.

E.A. Brown would have been in his element.

4/7/76

The Barnes boys...

Mechanics you can trust

The pickup developed a slight hesitation in the acceleration a while back to go along with its other infirmities. When you pressed on the pedal, gas sprayed over the motor, smoke poured from under the hood and the truck stood there trembling like a bird dog at point.

This constituted something of a safety hazard, since the truck is hard to get out of in the best of circumstances. The door on the driver's side was mashed in a couple of years ago by a Chapel Hill professor and you have to sit sideways on the seat, draw your knees up and kick it open.

As usual, I took it to Barnes's Garage for care. The co-proprietors, Donnie and Jaffey Barnes, are about the same age as my pickup and understand it better than anybody else.

It probably ought to be said that Barnes's is not your conventional garage. It is not even your conventional country garage.

To get there in the first place, you have to know already exactly where it is. The garage is on a deadend cutback off Lystra Church Road at the foot of Edwards Mountain. If you didn't know where it was, you would find it only by dumb luck, the way you might happen upon a well-situated liquor still.

The Barnes boys don't advertise and there is no sign about the place to indicate what it is. They depend on word-of-mouth through family, church and community connections.

They also depend on word-of-mouth to let folks know when the garage is open and doing business. This gets tricky because Barnes's has no set hours or days and frequently is closed for weeks at a time.

The arrangement must do pretty well because they always seem to have more work than they can handle. Donnie and Jaffey say so, anyway.

The garage itself is hidden by slash pines from Lystra Church Road traffic. It sits majestically among an admirable litter of rusting bodies, motors, wheels, axles and the like. Donnie once estimated there were 300 or so cars scattered about the premises proper and the adjoining pasture. He suggested, all in good fun, that my pickup belonged out there, too.

The garage building consists of four sides of sheet metal sort of propped up and held together by a slant roof of rough-cut lumber and tar paper. Inside, two shoulder-deep holes have been dug in the ground that Donnie and Jaffey call their pits.

There is a work table along one wall covered mostly with empty Pepsi bottles, cracker boxes and pork and beans cans. A small area at one end of the table is littered with bills and statements and other important papers and that is the "office." It is a rare experience when one of the Barneses first invites you to step into his office.

I checked the garage three or four times without hitting it right and finally, with the help of another regular customer, I lucked up on Jaffey at one of their tobacco barns. Donnie was hauling pulpwood that week and there was no telling when he would turn back into a mechanic.

Jaffey said to leave the pickup at the garage and he would look at it in a few days when he finished getting the tobacco barned. Sure enough he did, about a week or so later.

A few days after that, Jaffey drove the pickup to the house with his girl following in a cut-down, modified, gutted-muffler hybrid, the tail end riding about four feet off the ground and the whole thing looking and sounding like it would do 150 easy on a straight-away.

The financial transaction was what you might call delicate. Jaffey explained that he had practically rebuilt the motor and drive train, fine-tuned it, road-tested it three or four times on asphalt and gravel, and generally put it in track condition. He had also fixed the door so that it could be worked by hand instead of being kicked open.

Then he whimpered for a while about the sorry prices tobacco was bringing, the high cost of one thing and another, the prospect for a bitter winter, and the expense of getting married, which he was planning to do. At last he kicked the dirt a couple of times, squinted off into the middle distance and said, "That's gonna run you $6."

For some time after they left I kept thinking how wonderful things would be for the community if the Barnes boys would also start pumping gas.

12/8/74

At Doc Griffin's place...

Voting could be dangerous

An early Christmas present, a ceramic jackass, arrived in the mail last week and I was reminded right off of the November election.

The giver might not have meant for the jackass to be symbolic of the Democratic Party, but that was the way I chose to take it. Anyway, it wasn't the jackass that reminded me of the election. It was the ceramic as such.

Our polling place is in a little ceramics shop at the end of Lystra Church Road. Some might think it an unusual place to be exercising the privilege. That probably depends on what you've been used to.

Having attended two or three elections at the Eno Township precinct in Orange County, I would say the ceramics shop is a rather sophisticated polling place. I know it's a lot safer than Eno used to be.

Orange County has become a lot more civilized overall than it was when I attended elections there, and the Eno polling place has been moved to a less adventuresome location. The move was certainly sensible and in keeping with the democratic process, although it took some of the color and uncertainty out of the voting.

At the time I have in mind, the Eno polling place was located in Doc Griffin's service station on Highway 70.

Doc himself was a mild enough fellow when you got to know him. The thing that unnerved a lot of voters was that on election day, Doc would stroll around inside the place with a pistol hanging halfway out of his hip pocket. There were several Republican voters out there even then and they especially objected to the intimidating posture Doc struck. Of course, they had the wrong idea. They just didn't know him as well as the old-line Democrats, that was all.

Besides the Republicans, there were some Duke University people freshly settled in the township, and they didn't feel too comfortable with Doc's gun-toting either. Spending most of their time on the Duke campus, they probably didn't get to see pistols hanging out of hip pockets a whole lot.

Doc never pulled his pistol on a voter, Republican or Democrat, to my knowledge, although he did refuse to serve a few. So, the complaints about his rattling the voters were, to my mind, largely unjustified. The complainers kept whining about what could happen. Well, the service station could have been hit by a tornado on election day, as far as that went.

To be fair about it, Doc didn't pose nearly as much threat to orderly and free voting as the crowd that was always hanging about his place. Some of those fellows you would hesitate to walk by in bright sunshine with a police escort.

They clustered around the doorway, sitting on Pepsi crates and Doc's cane-bottom chairs, forming a downright surly phalanx. If a voter didn't look exactly right — that is, if the voter didn't look like he belonged in Eno Township — they would make uncouth remarks to one another or maybe spit tobacco juice where he was getting ready to step and generally let him know that voting wasn't the best idea he'd ever had.

For all of that, I never heard of any real election day trouble at Doc's until the early 1960s. I was trying to get the Eno vote count for an anxious candidate in the primary and kept calling and calling without getting an answer. Finally, around one o'clock in the morning, I called the sheriff's office, which was election headquarters.

One of the deputies said they were fighting in Doc's place about the tally and as soon as it was over somebody was going out there. The deputy didn't mean they were arguing about the count. He meant fighting.

As I understand it, some constitutional law professors from Duke got the State Board of Elections all wrought up and that was what finished Doc Griffin's as the polling place.

12/11/74

Baptists vote no...

Immersion issue sinks again

The Baptist State Convention has once again, for the fourth year running, drowned the immersion issue, and I am again left with sorely mixed emotions.

The proposal before the convention this year, just like those for the last three years, called for expulsion of churches that accept members from other denominations without requiring them to be baptized in a good immersion. Eleven churches in the convention leave immersion to personal preference, and they would have been expelled had the proposal been approved. As you know, the proposal sank with barely a ripple.

Living down here in what is generally regarded as the liberal end of Chatham County and only a few miles from Chapel Hill, I have to stand up now and again for personal preference, or the unfettered pursuit of truth and happiness, as they say at the university.

Still, as a Baptist who has been in and out of the denomination with disconcerting frequency and been dipped more times than I can say with precision, I have a warm spot for immersion. Hence, the sorely mixed emotions.

To the best of my recollection, I joined the Baptist church five times — first in northern Orange County, three times in Durham, and the last time out here at Lystra. Over the years I have also joined the Methodist Church (twice), the Presbyterian church, and once almost became a High Episcopalian.

I am not really all that flighty about my church membership. In my youth I got into the habit of joining my girl friend's church, to make the relationship seem complete, and then found that it was much simpler to change girl friends and churches than it was to patch up arguments.

I missed out on High Episcopal because the pastor took a dim view of my church history. He said it would be wise to wait a while and ponder on it, and sure enough it was. Before long I found myself going with a regular Methodist.

The best baptizings I ever took part in or just witnessed were those held in the Eno River in northern Orange. I remember one in particular that I watched from the bank of the Mighty Eno, and I never saw such carrying-on in my life.

The pastor was dressed in frock coat over bib overalls, winged collar and black string tie. He stood out there in midstream, about waist-deep, with more aplomb than you would have thought possible under the circumstances. All the women to be dipped were dressed in white. The men wore nondescript, it being in the Depression and clothes hard to buy.

Each one to be baptized carried a white handkerchief. The pastor held the handkerchief over each supplicant's mouth and nose and then flopped her (or him) over backwards in a sort of half-gainer.

The baptized would come up dripping and blowing and more often than not would say something to the pastor, in which case he would take them under again. On that particular Sunday afternoon it seemed like every one of them was triple-dipped.

All the while this was going on, the members of the flock spread along the bank sang and clapped and moaned and shouted their amens. When the baptizing was done, everybody fell upon the fried chicken and fixings and had a fine time. Although I didn't get baptized myself that time, one of the few I let go by in those days, I did join in on the chicken. (To give you a full report, the fishing on that stretch of the Mighty Eno wasn't worth fooling with for the next several days.)

These days, of course we are much more sophisticated. Most of your Baptist churches of any size have built-in tanks, usually up there behind the pulpit, for baptizings.

We don't have a tank at Lystra yet, although one is being figured in the long-range building plans. In the meantime, Lystra borrows the tank at Mt. Gilead, a few miles down the road.

When I joined Lystra a while back, the pastor asked me if I would like to be baptized again. The church had another big one coming up.

I've still got a stiff knee and a bum shoulder from a fall a year ago and I told him no. I thought I'd let this one go. I hope the folks who brought forth the proposal at the Baptist State Convention will understand.

11/24/74

Take it from an expert...

Good luck, organic farmers

That was an inspiring story, the one about the 22-year-old Gastonia bricklayer and his beloved going into farming after learning the ways of the land under the tutelage of the National Sharecroppers Fund.

The recounting of how Mike Carpenter and Lorraine Walker, who by now is Mrs. Carpenter, learned to till the soil brought tears to my eyes. Mike and Lorraine took the organic way, using turkey and chicken manure and other exotic materials in the place of commercial fertilizer to replenish the barren acreage of the Frank Porter Graham farm near Wadesboro.

I can discourse on this agricultural phenomenon with some authority, since I happen to be a former organic farmer. Looking down my own days of slinging manure and sorting out garbage for the compost pile was what brought tears to my eyes.

The old girl and I started organic farming our place in Chatham County with high hopes and considerable zest. Our enthusiasm was practically bounding for folks our age, which is a good deal more than 22.

When we started out, the old girl saved garbage with spirit. Besides accumulating our own leavings, she got garbage from the two married daughters on promise of sharing the crop. I sorted out the bounty, putting the cans, bottles, cartons and other non-biodegradables into the regular garbage cans, and hauling the natural fertilizer to the compost pile. The sparse contents of the regular cans led the garbageman to observe with some pique, "You folks sure clean your plates good." He was put out, naturally, because he had hogs at home to feed.

I built that compost pile the winter-long, spicing it periodically with manure from Sam's stall, and garnishing the whole mess with nice layers of lime. Not to brag, but the quality of the compost was striking. You could track that stuff across a rug and it would defy all of your brand-name shampoos. Lye would eat it off, but nothing else touched it. Guests encountering a tracked rug would sniff, look kind of sideways and smile thinly.

By March, we seemed to have attracted all the flies in the area. March is a little early for that many flies even in Chatham. On a sunny day, with the flies droning and the delicate aroma of rotting garbage wafting about, our place was a tourist attraction of a sort. We attracted possums, stray dogs and cats, and the district sanitation officer. He said he was conducting soil percolation tests, although I'm certain in my own mind he noticed the haze that seemed to hang above the compost pile through sunshine, cold and rain.

When the children started coming home later and later from school, the old girl suggested that it might be a good idea to spread the compost in the garden. By the time I finished transferring the compost from the pile to the garden, my olfactory nerves were shot and my tear ducts gone dry, so it didn't bother me any more. But others, including the old girl whose judgment I trust, claimed I had created a regular miasma in exposing the bottom of the pile to soft breezes and sun. The old girl suggested that I turn the compost under.

The organic garden was what you could call reluctant. Our corn grew knee-high and stopped while the stand across the road leaped high as an elephant's eye. The beefsteak tomatoes got to the size of a student dining hall meatball and then died, presumably of shame. We had the nicest squash, cucumber, watermelon and cantaloupe vines in the community. No squash, cucumbers, watermelons, or cantaloupes to speak of, just vines.

True to the last jot and tittle of pure organic farming, we scorned all insecticides, herbicides, dusts and sprays. The bugs, beetles, birds, nematodes, blights and wilts seemed to appreciate that very much. I did, too. It was quite an experience to stand there, leaning on a hoe, and see a tomato plant disappear right in front of your eyes.

That was our introduction and farewell to organic farming. The next season we went the conventional way, using commercial fertilzer, insecticides, everything the garden store could spare. The crop turned out pretty good. The tomatoes, counting the price of the plants, fertilizer, spray and labor, only cost us about $4 apiece.

I wish Mike and Lorraine Carpenter well. Personally, given a choice, I would take bricklaying, on which I can discourse with equal authority.
10/27/74

III
LIFE IN THE COUNTRY
(Orange County)

She had a special talent...

Fishing with old granny

Fishing, like toe dancing, playing the violin and piano, must be learned at a tender age if it is to be productive, artistic and deeply satisfying to the soul. Even then nothing is guaranteed.

I started early, at my grandmother's knee, and occasionally, when a moccasin slid through the water, in her lap.

Our fishing trips began in the hog pen or the pasture or behind the smokehouse, where grubworms could be found beneath the trough, under rocks and cowflops. The bait box was a tin can filled with moist black loam. Provisions for us were a couple of apples, a Mason jar of well water and a can of Tube Rose for old Granny.

She was nearing 70 then and liked her dip of snuff, for comfort and to aim, sometimes with great accuracy, at water snakes. She switched to chewing gum later on her doctor's orders.

Those were trying times, and one of the rules for survival was not to buy anything that could be got without cost from the homeplace and environs. So, instead of fiberglass rods or cane poles, we used hickory branches. Instead of nylon or monofilament lines, we had odd pieces of string and twine saved from Christmas packages and mail-order arrivals. The floats were cork stoppers from her bottles of Black Draught and Lydia E. Pinkham's.

The only cash outlay, a dime or so, was for hooks. She never lost one with good grace to a fighting fish. The dismay wasn't at the fish that got away but at the hook long gone.

Our favorite fishing hole was in a creek, a tributary of the Mighty Eno, running alongside the railroad tracks. The water ran cool and clear, and sitting on the bank you could see a perch or cat nuzzling the grubworm and wondering whether to take a bite.

The last time I looked for the fishing hole I was parked on a bridge and, peering down through the dapplings of sunshine and shadow, saw only mudflats and garbage, with a thin brown trickle coursing through the litter. Not even a mudcat would have risked it.

Old Granny talked to the fish, softening the rasp she used on wayward children: "Come on now, honey, take a little nibble for Miss Florrie." In the ignorance of my callow youth, I didn't know whether the fish heard her siren song, but sometimes they seemed to, taking the bait at her cooing.

I have tried a roughly similar technique in the Caswell surf, railing at the fish and threatening terrible vengeance if they didn't hit the bait. The results have been mixed. One time I hooked the stump of an old piling and another time a woman moved her children out of earshot.

When old Granny wasn't talking to the fish or juicing water snakes with the Tube Rose or humming Baptist standards — her lifelong favorites were "Amazing Grace" and "Just As I Am" and "Bringing In The Sheaves" — she bowed to the teachings of Jeremiah and tried to bend the tree, meaning me, in the way that it should grow.

She lectured, sometimes with appropriate Biblical injunctions and sometimes with horrible examples, on the virtues of honesty, cleanliness, godliness, thrift, hard work, patience, tolerance, good manners, proper meals and sound sleep.

Her guiding principle, one that I didn't understand then and have puzzled over since, was that everyone ought to find his station in life and stick to it. Her harshest indictment of one who had failed miserably at work, marriage or life in general was that he had tried to rise above his station or sunk beneath it.

Sometimes when the fishing is rotten and the nature is restless and the urge is strong to move on, to another house, another place, another clime, another calling, I remember old Granny and smile at the memory and hold my ground.

8/11/85

Increasing indignities...

Painful changes mar memories

I used to try to go up there every spring, to northern Orange County whence my forebears sprang, to see what new indignity had been visited upon that once pastoral land. This time there had been a four-year interlude and, even though I am as willing as the next one to accept change, I wasn't ready for headlong transmogrification.

For a while, there seemed reason to hope for the best, maybe a re-ruralization of the territory along the lines of an early Wyeth or a Timberlake — old barns weathering gracefully, farm houses going genteely to seed and split-rail fences coming to final rest. Dogwoods were in bloom and the hardwoods were showing life, and across the fields, a couple of open ones that were left, yellow wildflowers lent a nice touch.

The first disenchantment came where the old University Station used to be — or where I figured it used to be. Mobile homes had overwhelmed the community. There wasn't a trace of the old train station or general store/ post office, not even a crumbled chimney.

One of the last houses still standing, built by my grandmother and inherited half a century ago by my mother, was barely intact, gutted and empty now, ready to go to dust. Across the tracks, about where the old water tower stood, was a new billboard announcing: 31 acres — Prime Development Land — Almega Homes and Investments.

I walked along the spur track for a couple of hundred yards to where I figured the depot had been and looked in vain for at least the stump of a magnificent weeping willow that had stood in the side yard. Nothing suggested that anything had even been there. I picked up half a dozen rusty spikes to use as paperweights and maybe to keep the memory evergreen.

At the turnoff from the old Highway 70 into University Station Road, Doc Griffin's fabled service station, where Democrats used to come to blows on election day over vote counts, was now the Buy Quick Food Mart. A banner out front announced movie rentals. I didn't bother to go in, Doc being long dead.

The Mount Hermon Baptist Church cemetery had been completely enclosed with a hurricane fence, for sound reason. The land next to the cemetery was being cleared for a grand mobile home park.

They were all still in their regular resting places — parents, grand-parents, great-grandparents, aunts, uncles, cousins, other kin several times removed — although it took me a while to get my bearings with the new population explosion.

Across the road, the original site of the church, only a sweeping lawn now, also had been fenced, giving a demarcation between the new beer distributorship alongside.

Across Highway 70, down Pleasant Green Road, a misnomer now if there ever was one, upscale houses in the $150,000 range had sprung up where once there had been hard scrabble family farms and barely enough to eat, although world enough and time.

Pleasant Green United Methodist Church had suddenly doubled in size, with a new education building to the rear of the sanctuary where in my youth I had dozed Sunday mornings away.

My forebears were neatly divided by denomination — paternal ancestors all Baptists, maternal all Methodists — as well as by Highway 70 — Shumakers on the south side, Cardens on the north. I never understood exactly how my mother and father first got together, neither of them having spent much time in school.

The entryway, barely a trail now, to my maternal grandparents' home place and the family cemetery where they lay, had a cable stretched across it and a sign saying No Trespassing. I got out of the car and was standing there deliberating whether to hike down the trail when a Jeep Cherokee roared down the road, leaving me with a nice layer of Orange County's red dust.

So, I said the heck with it and left, maybe for good this time. It doesn't pay to try to go back.

4/9/89

Attic search inspires...

Scenes from the distant past

I was in the attic looking for a string of Christmas tree lights and puttering around in the family debris that had collected through the years; the photographs turned up in an album, flaked and yellowed with age.

The land in northern Orange County then was gently rolling with red clay stretches divided by single-strand barbed-wire fences, the river and marked rocks and hedgerows, and was green with pines and hardwoods and sweetgums and scented by honeysuckle.

The land is still gently rolling except where the bulldozers have slashed, and now there are trailer courts and Jim Walter houses and a convenience store. The river is now a shallow creek and has the consistency of a thin mud soup.

One old photograph showed Theo and his girl, Bertha — Theo in a tunic buttoned to the chin and Sam Browne belt, Bertha in a lacy white ankle-length frock, the height of fashion in 1918. They were smiling tentatively, sitting in a flat-bottom rowboat at midstream, giving the impression of young and tender innocence momentarily arrested.

Another photograph showed the land under snow. The distinctive feature was the railroad track, the permanent link to Durham and Hillsborough and Carrboro, or so it must have seemed at the time.

A photograph probably taken at the same time showed Theo in the snow beside the depot, capped and knickered, with a proprietary air, holding the bridle of a billy-goat hitched to a sled filled with children.

The depot was a complex: general store with the post office cage in one corner; waiting room with two benches and a pot-bellied wood stove and another cage for the station agent; the baggage room, usually with boxes of chicks cheeping; living quarters to the rear; and fronting all of this, a platform.

The young Theo pushed the baggage carts along the platform and lugged in the mail pouch flung from a door of the train that merely slowed when there was nothing else to disgorge and no passengers to board.

Life had seemed uncomplicated then, Theo said later.

His glimpse of the outside world came from the newspapers dropped daily by the train and the magazines and periodicals in the post office.

There was no photograph of his mother, Flora, in the old album. I didn't need one; my memory of her was vivid. Her first article of faith, after the Lord and the Baptist church, was work. While her first husband talked politics, his main calling, she plowed, sowed and harvested, bore their children, including Theo, and ran the general store and post office and depot.

She was tart-tongued and iron-willed and might have seemed to be without sentiment or tenderness. But there were moments that gave her away.

Once, I saw her standing beside the weeping willow in the station yard, bonnet brim turned back to give her face to the evening sun, gnarled hands clenched and rammed into her apron pockets, watching the flyer come through. Long after the train passed she continued standing there gazing into the distance, and in her expression was something sad and yearning, or so I thought, surprised to find it in that hard old woman.

Theo escaped at 17, to Durham briefly and a job that he mentioned only vaguely and then to the army and World War I, which he talked about not at all. The army and World War I accounted for the tunic and Sam Browne belt in the old photograph.

I never did find the string of lights for the Christmas tree.

12/18/83

In Granny's Orange County...

Simpler times forgotten

A couple of Sundays ago we drove up into northern Orange County, 20 miles or so distant, and in a way I wish I hadn't gone.

The trip was mainly to measure a headstone in the old Mt. Hermon Baptist Church cemetery so we could get a matching one for the new grave. There was nothing funereal about the journey. The burial was six months ago.

Part of the county is the way it always has been, gently rolling with red clay rises and falls. Along the stretches the developers haven't gotten to yet, the pines and cedars and hardwoods and hollies and dogwoods march right up to the shoulders and you still feel that strange loneliness peculiar to southern rural roads on a Sunday afternoon.

The old cemetery seems out of place and time. The familiar Orange County names, many of them reaching back beyond the Regulators, are still there, on the headstones. But that is about all there is to take you back.

The old church building has long since been succeeded by a grander edifice on another road and there is not even a chimney rubble to mark where it stood.

The railroad track, also out of time and place, still runs alongside the cemetery. Invariably, it seemed, in memory anyway, the funerals of my boyhood were accompanied by an engine's long and lonely whistle in the distance. Sometimes on Sunday mornings the clickety-clack of the wheels on the rails would give a metronome effect to "Amazing Grace" ringing in the rafters. Now the roadbed is going to weeds and the rails to rust and instead of the lonely whistle you hear the hiss of traffic along the interstate a couple of hundred yards away.

On the way back we turned onto the road where University Station used to be, a couple of miles from the cemetery, closer if you walk the tracks, although nobody would dream of doing that now. In the old days that was where Chapel Hill students changed trains to take the spur line to Carrboro.

The station itself was a complex, general store with the post office cage in one corner; waiting room with benches and a wood stove and another cage with a telegraph key and timetables and tickets and a desk for the station agent; baggage room with, always it seemed, boxes of chicks cheeping away. Fronting all of this was a long porch with ramps at each end and that was the favorite place to sit and watch the locals letting off and taking on passengers if there were any and the through trains streaking by, sometimes hurling out a pouch of mail on the fly.

My grandmother ran it all, the general store and post office, and the station itself as interim agent. The regular agents seemed to come and go almost as regularly as the trains and when in residence they tended to sink into their cups. The solitude of the job made wandering and drinking occupational hazards.

I spent some golden days there, watching the trains, sneaking horehound candy and dried apples out of the store, going through people's mail, and fleeing my grandmother's rough hand and tart tongue.

It was a simpler time for us, partly because our field of vision was short and narrow, reaching only to the upgrade to the west and the bend in the rails to the east.

There is no longer a trace. Even the neat hedges that bordered the station yard are gone, along with a magnificent weeping willow. The whole area has been turned into a trailer court.

The name itself is gone. Officially it is no longer University Station. A green marker beside the tracks proclaims it to be Glenn. The final desecration.

There is another store across the tracks now where the water tower used to stand, catering to the trailer court. I remarked to the fellow behind the counter that the place sure had changed and he said, "How do you mean?" There didn't seem to be much point in trying to explain.
11/10/74

Consultants' studies not needed...

Hearings detect hayseed hostility

Orange County's commissioners, all of them urbanites and suburbanites to the marrow, have just spent thousands of dollars to find out what I could have told them free of charge.

The expensive discovery is that rural residents of Orange, those living out in the boondocks and coming to town only for provisions and maybe gainful employment, don't have much use for city folks. Some of them don't mind having city dwellers around for two or three minutes at a time, to laugh at when they come into country stores to ask directions or where they can buy some good land cheap. Any more than that and the rustics' merriment quickly subsides.

The Orange commissioners also found out that the rustics don't have much use for county commissioners, either, looking at them askance, with knit brows and clenched teeth, when they have to look at them at all, which they had just as soon not do, given a choice.

Besides being deeply suspicious of the commissioners and almost all other county officials, with the notable exception of the sheriff, who can sit next to a pot-bellied stove and squirt tobacco juice and talk country with the best of them, the hayseeds hate zoning. (I call them hayseeds with a certain affection, having been one before taking on all my Chapel Hill polish, and having come from a long line of them.)

To the hayseed mind, county zoning, the peculiar government practice of telling a landowner what he can and can't do with his own property, smacks of communism, dictatorship, socialism and cruel and unusual punishment. Some zoners, going clean beyond the bounds of decency and all under-standing, would make an honest, God-fearing, morally erect, family-loving landholder get rid of his hog pens, compost pile and chicken rendering operation, for crying out loud.

The rural attitudes in Orange were turned up by a consulting firm in a series of public hearings. The findings will be used to try to serve rural areas in case there are any left after Chapel Hill gets through growing like a weed and Carrboro and Hillsborough finish putting on municipal airs, annexing everything in sight.

At one of the hearings a native hayseed pointed to one of his neighbors and said, "That person is from our area, but he's one of *them*," meaning that the neighbor was a confounded newcomer. A bona fide Orange Countian is one whose parents and grandparents were born in Orange and never left the county, except maybe for military service and then returning thereafter forthwith. All others, regardless of the years in residence, are newcomers.

The public hearings also turned up the startling discovery that the rustics aren't fond of PhDs and academicians of lesser rank, down to teaching assistants, especially those who wander out from Duke and Chapel Hill. They will restrain their disaffection long enough to sell the academics some vegetables or a cord of wood or a vealer. Sometimes one in desperate financial straits will sell a PhD yearning for the country life a couple of

acres of cut-over, played-out, gullied and rock-strewn land unfit for tim-
bering or tilling or grazing or even gazing upon except sideways. The
sudden windfall doesn't make the rustic feel kindly toward the academic,
just vastly amused.

When I lived down in the Chatham County boondocks, where the rural
attitudes are identical to those in Orange, I used to tell people I was on
relief, which wasn't far from the truth, to keep from admitting that I had
anything to do with Chapel Hill. If anybody said anything about the
campus parking sticker, I always said, "Oh, that. I stole that car." My
neighbors down there could tolerate a car thief in their midst with a lot
more grace than they could a Chapel Hill academic.

One of them caught me red-handed one day down at the barn grading
students' papers. That's when I knew it was time to move.
2/12/89

And so their lot has ever been...

Farm women knew only toil

A sociologist at the University in Chapel Hill has in a way discovered
fire, finding that women are the strong backbone of America's family
farms, those that are still operating.

A national survey showed women handling the bookkeeping, holding
outside jobs and doing farm chores, not to mention bearing and raising
children, cooking and canning, housekeeping, gardening, sewing, shopping, doing the weekly wash and holding circle meetings. Those were the
designated duties and did not take in psychological counseling, tutoring,
moral instruction and the like.

They performed throughout their waking hours largely without recognition or much appreciation or even self-awareness. They go, most of them,
from wedding bells to the grave without ever having been remarked as a
marvel of sorts, except by sociologists sorting out the human condition.

I know the type well and can say with authority that, even though the
survey was conducted in this day and age, the farm woman's lot has ever
been thus.

Both of my grandmothers were farm women. In an absolute sense. If family recollections are accurate, one of them never ventured beyond the metes and bounds of the farm throughout her married life except to attend Sunday services and other church functions.

She bore her children in her own bed, suffered her miseries there, and finally died there. Her view of the world was bounded mainly by kitchen, sewing table, wash-tub, garden, henhouse, smokehouse, corncrib, barn, well, and the piney woods beyond the pastures.

Even in death she remained on a short tether — buried in the family graveyard, a clod's throw from the front porch.

The idea of the place continuing to function as a family farm without her omnipresence was far-fetched, as it turned out. With her death, her husband, my grandfather, suffered a pronounced lack of direction and the family scattered like flushed quail.

The last time I saw the place, a couple of years ago, broomstraw and scrub pine and kudzu had taken over. The only sign left of those years of toil was the family cemetery. Even her gravestone was blank, the epitaph worn away by 58 years of weathering.

My other grandmother was cosmopolitan by comparison, but still a true farm woman, of necessity and by inclination. She survived two husbands, neither of them worth shooting for any practical purpose except procreation.

Her "outside jobs," as the sociologist put it, consisted of running a general store, serving as postmistress and railroad station agent, landlording it over her rental properties and, in the early years, spending her evenings turning and stringing tobacco sacks for Golden Belt Manufacturing Company in Durham.

She was bound only by the limits of where she had a mind to go, her husbands having no say in the matter: to Durham by mules and wagon for supplies for the general store; to Hillsborough, and the county seat, to have the mules shod and for registering deeds; and occasionally to Greensboro, by train, for meetings in her role as station agent.

The outside jobs provided her treasure and the wherewithal to satisfy her land lust. But her heart was in the fields, behind the plow, in the pigpen chasing shoats, killing hogs in the fall, scattering corn for chickens and later wringing their necks, and on her knees in the garden mothering shoots to growth.

Both of those women, one with a gentle spirit and compliant nature as restful and comforting as a feather pillow after a hard day, and the other flinty and tart and driven by personal demons that in her most reflective moments she never discussed and maybe never even examined, were not merely the strong backbones of their family farms; they were heart and soul and to a large extent, the muscle.

On the whole, I would say the sociologist's findings are sound.

8/31/86

An attack on 'castle' principle...

Governmental nitpicking

The latest frontal attack on the democratic principle and constitutional guarantee that a man's home is his castle, safe from government nitpicking, proves conclusively that the country is going to hell in a handbasket or maybe an attache case.

I refer, of course, to the governmental harassment of John Davis and his roosters in Historical Hillsborough, often called these days Hysterical Hillsborough. This was just one more instance in the long list of denials of life, liberty and the pursuit of happiness.

A while back, it was pigs. Catherine Redding fell victim to the bureaucracy of Rochester, NY, on account of her Yorkshire pig, named C.D., for Christmas Dinner. The city court and the Humane Society conspired to get C.D. kicked out of Ms. Redding's house and into the slaughterhouse.

Then there was the municipal oppression of Steve Kenney in Kenmore, NY. A naturalist and admirer of Henry David Thoreau, Kenney went to some expense, $35, to plant his lawn in wildflowers. He quit mowing the lawn for environmental and aesthetic reasons.

The building inspector said Kenney's natural lawn didn't fit in with the neighborhood concept. The town attorney said the height of the lawn, five feet, created a safety problem, because children could get lost in there, and several other municipal codes were being broken.

Kenney replied, in an oration that would have pleased Thoreau, Thomas Paine and Patrick Henry: "Where does a community's power end? Part of the whole American idea is the concept of diversity and accommodation of individual rights. Beauty is in the eye of the beholder and I happen to prefer wildflowers to grass."

Then there was the unconscionable municipal attack by Coral Gables, FL, on Keith Catambay, a carpenter who works out of a rusting van. He parked it overnight in front of his house.

Coral Gables invoked an ordinance that imposes fines up to $250 a day on those who park commercial vans or pickups in residential areas where they can be seen with the naked eye. Catambay said, reasonably, "This law is stupid."

Getting back to the roosters in Hillsborough, John Davis, the owner, is a self-described down-to-earth, good old country boy, even though he lives in town. He keeps two roosters as pets and for rural verisimilitude.

Each dawn the roosters crow, as roosters will, waking up the neighborhood. Neighbors complained and the town adopted an ordinance banning roosters except in ovens and on the table.

In a fine lament Davis said: "It's not the chickens. I don't care that much about chickens. It's the principle of the thing." Then, harking back to his country rearing, he went on to say, "I wouldn't trade it for nothing – getting up, fixing a cup of coffee and listening to the roosters crowing."

The victimization of John Davis, along with the other outrages, not only is deeply depressing but, especially in Davis' case, startling. I can remember when Hillsborough financed most of its municipal government with a mayor's traffic court and single stoplight. About the only thing anybody could do to offend municipal order and the sense of the fitness of things was to skip town without paying off traffic tickets.

The social whirl was around the courthouse and a blacksmith shop specializing in shoeing mules and a pool hall where you could get away with sipping from Mason jars.

Anybody thinking about outlawing crowing or denying roosters, hens and pullets the run of the town would have been checked for rabies.
7/19/87

Hold community identity...

Save the rural post offices

The word from Washington that the federal government might stop shutting down the country's rural post offices, as if they were bawdy houses or liquor stills, is heartening news.

Rep. Keith Sebelius, R-KS, had it about right when he told the General Accounting Office: "When a community loses its post office, it also loses its identity." Nobody has asked me to testify, but I can offer direct evidence to support Rep. Sebelius's view.

My grandmother used to run one of those rural post offices back in the twenties and thirties, years before automation, stamp machines and zip codes.

Her post office was a cage-like affair in the corner of the general store, which she also ran. The general store adjoined the train depot, and she ran the depot, too. The whole operation was located at University Station, a crossroads community in Orange County. My grandmother also ran the community, or tried to.

There were only three good reasons to go to University Station: to get on the train or sit and watch them go by; to buy provisions at the general store, or to do business with the post office. People also used to go there to vote, but I don't count that as a good reason. Everybody knew the community would go Democratic anyway.

The post office had a swivel chair, scarred desk and rows of pigeonholes for sorting mail. I spent a lot of time in the swivel chair munching horehound candy and pretending to conduct official business. Later on, after learning to read, I went through the mail keeping track of what was going and coming. My grandmother also let me operate the cancellation stamp once I had learned to ink it properly, although that was probably against regulations.

The post office also served as a bank of sorts, with people putting their spare cash in Postal Savings. That's something you never hear about nowadays, Postal Savings, and it was No. 3 in my grandmother's trinity. As she saw it, salvation rested in the Baptist Church, and the Democratic Party, and Postal Savings. With the possible exception of Postal Savings, I am inclined to agree.

University Station might have had some identity without the post office, since it was a train stop and all the UNC students got off there to take the spur line to Carrboro. The only other way to get to Chapel Hill was on a terrible road from Durham and nobody in his right mind would have taken it voluntarily.

But the post office was what gave University Station its real throb and attracted much of its commerce. Practically the whole community turned out to watch the mail train come through, to see the canvas bag come hurtling out of the post office car, and then wait for my grandmother to sort. They didn't cut up like front-line soldiers, at mail-call, but they weren't nonchalant about it either. There was a certain air of expectancy, you might say.

I'm sure my grandmother took a quiet pride in the University Station cancellation stamp, although she never made any commotion about it. She never made any commotion about anything except children getting out of line and the country going Republican. Validating train tickets with the University Station stamp swelled her pride too, but that was minor compared with the joy of banging down on a letter, knowing that it might carry the name of University Station clear across the country.

The train depot burned in the late 1940s, I think it was, carrying the general store and the post office with it, and nothing was ever replaced. The site is now occupied by a row of mobile homes.

There is no University Station post office anymore; there is not even a University Station. The community is now named Glenn, proving exactly what Rep. Sebelius told the government.
9/28/75

A campaign tip...

Helms needs 'Amazing Grace'

The first time I heard "Amazing Grace" was more than half a century ago, in the original Mount Hermon Baptist Church, in northern Orange County.

The piano player/choir director and the preacher used "Amazing Grace" regularly for the invitation, even though in hard-shell Baptist terminology it is a hymn of salvation.

I could sit in Mount Hermon and let the benedictions and prayers and sermons wash over me and the collection plate pass by, rising when my grandmother thumped me, sitting when she pushed me back down, without rousing from my semi-stupor.

But when the preacher said turn to page 188 in the hymnals for "Amazing Grace," the hairs stood out on the back of my neck, the way it does for some when they sing "America the Beautiful" and "We Shall Overcome."

The congregation, a solemn and somnolent lot for the most part, rang the rafters with that fine old hymn. They threw themselves vigorously into "Rock of Ages" and "Blest Be the Tie That Binds" and "Just As I Am," nearly drowning out the freights clattering down the tracks a hundred yards to the south. But for getting into the spirit of the thing nothing came close to "Amazing Grace."

The congregation at Mount Hermon was made up almost entirely of Scotch-Irish and German stock. They were scratch-farmers and small merchants and none of them, so far as I knew, had sprung from slavers or slave-holders. The idea, let alone the practice, wouldn't have struck them.

If they had known that "Amazing Grace" was composed by John Newton, an old slave-ship captain, their enthusiasm for the hymn might have been tempered, but I doubt it. They would have clung to "Amazing Grace," I expect, even if Catholics and High Episcopalians sang it.

In later years I became a constant of sorts in the choir at the old Lystra Baptist Church, in Chatham County. The choir director always wound up practice on Wednesday nights with freedom of choice. I tried to be ready, sitting there in a half-crouch, and more often than not got in first with a call for "Amazing Grace." After a while everybody had it down by heart.

My collection of "Amazing Grace" records once ranged from Ella Fitzgerald to the Black Watch bagpipers. The records are all gone now, given away, loaned, lost in moves from one place to another, and it is too late to start over; but I can still call back when I want to the sound of those bagpipes wailing and Ella bending the notes in a way that would have startled Captain Newton.

I mention all of this because, as far as I'm concerned, it sheds an entirely new light on Sen. Jesse Helms. In a survey by a Virginia church, Jesse revealed that his favorite hymn was "Amazing Grace." He said it brought back memories of his father. Anybody who can remember his father in that particular light must be at least semi-redeemed.

7/10/83

IV
LIFE ON THE COAST

Here's how Thoreau felt...

Progress hits Caswell Beach

When we started coming down here between my first and second childhoods, Oak Island was still getting its second growth, in the way that a cut-over forest primeval starts coming back.

The original development of the island had been virtually wiped out in 1954 by Hurricane Hazel. Only three or four structures out of about 365 were left standing. The others had been reduced to splinters, flotsam and jetsam, or tossed by wind and waves across the Intracoastal, some into treetops on the mainland.

In the late 1950s and early 1960s the island was still trying to get even. Businesses and cottages were coming back, slowly.

On Caswell Beach, which has always been, through careful planning and lucky circumstance, notably retarded in development, the march to today's residential squeeze has been snail-like. The careful planning was simply gritty determination not to let business of any kind get a toehold. The lucky circumstance, holding for many years, was the presence at Fort Caswell of the Baptist Assembly, which owned the waterline and was able to control indirectly all development.

In those days the few cottages available on Caswell were rented by an old soul who lived beside the lighthouse and ran a casual operation. An ocean-front cottage that now brings upwards of $1,000 a week went for less than $100.

The Caswell Beach Road sometimes was tricky, lengths of it disappearing under sand in a good northeaster. Along some stretches you would see only sand dunes and the windblown yaupon and live oak.

The only nighttime activity on Caswell was the beam from the lighthouse sweeping the area and an occasional church activity bus trundling along the road to the Baptist Assembly grounds at the fort.

It was easy to get the feeling at any of the island's three beaches — Caswell, Yaupon and Long Beach — of being in a marine semi-wilderness, such was the peace and quiet and easy pace and comparative isolation. Those who knew and appreciated the old days and ways are now seeing, as they put it, the whole area going straight to hell.

This spring the Beach Road, the mainland causeway leading to the bridge across the Intracoastal, sprang from two lanes to three. The second shopping center on the causeway plunged into Phase II. A Kentucky Fried Chicken is blooming, joining in the fast-food panoply of McDonald's, Pizza Inn, Western Sizzlin', Hardee's and some I have probably left out accidentally, meaning no slight.

Also among the recent and new arrivals on the causeway, civilizing the area, you might say, are a used car lot, a discount furniture house, a bicycle dealership, a household appliance store, two miniature golf courses (one for adults and one for certifiable children), an ice cream parlor, knick-knacks shop (bringing the total in the immediate area to several dozen) and a chain supermarket (replacing one that called it a day).

Long Beach has just installed a traffic light, its first, not counting the yellow caution light that used to blink at the main intersection. Yaupon got the first traffic light on the island a few months ago and now, in a municipal race that figures to leave everyone breathless, is conspiring to widen its main street to three lanes, the middle one for turning only, no passing.

Here on Caswell, where there used to be those long open spaces, only two or three marsh-front lots are left, the cheapest going for a tidy $66,000. On the ocean-front, a lot that was quoted at $600 right after Hurricane Hazel and went begging can still be had, for $175,000. Only a couple are left.

Across the way, on Bald Head Island where the gentry play, a telephone system has been installed, with a microwave tower in the marine forest and underground lines, for crying out loud.

I think I know how Thoreau must have felt when the first picnickers showed up at Walden Pond.

5/22/88

Here's dollar documentation

Boat: hole to pour money into

A saltwater sage on Oak Island advised everybody within hearing distance a few years ago of the folly of owning a boat for any reason except gainful employment or maybe to escape a nuclear disaster.

For those on Oak Island, the possibility of a nuclear disaster is somewhat more than a laughing matter since the only escape route other than by water leads straight toward the maw of Carolina Power & Light's nuclear plant.

"A boat," the sage practically hollered in Mort's Barber Shop, "is nothing but a hole in the water that you pour money into." Mort's is closed now and the building has been put up for sale, but not on account of the fellow's hollering. Mort retired and moved in with his children near Myrtle Beach, I hear.

It turned out the bottom of the fellow's boat, a 17-footer, had to be scraped and painted. The paint and all came to $900, and with the scraping and labor and dry-dockage, he had to peel off roughly $1,500.

The marine paint, he explained, ran $300 a gallon, substantially more than he paid for Jack Daniels'. He held up a half-pint, which I assumed he carried around for demonstration purposes, and hollered, "Know what this little baby costed? Twenty-two ninety-five, that's what." ("Costed" is acceptable usage, widely admired for its clarity, on Oak Island.)

I about halfway listened to the harangue. Sometimes I wish I had paid stricter attention.

My son and his wife, professional clammers, and I, a rank amateur, are on our third boat in a year and a half. Two of the boats are sort of dry-docked in their front yard. The latest one is still operational.

The first one sold to us by a retiree who claimed he had taken it out only on Sundays and then only to give the motor a light workout, was a 14-foot skiff with a 15-hp motor, barely enough power to manage tidal creeks and the Intracoastal on a nice day.

The hull was sound enough but the motor was temperamental, demanding 50 or 60 pulls to cough into action and long rest periods at awkward times, like out on the briny with storm clouds piling up.

We decided to put the skiff on standby, as an emergency reserve, and went next to an 18-foot Glasspar with an 85-hp Evinrude, a practical workboat without any frills except for the windshield and seats.

That baby would move, cutting a good wake and handling as nicely as anybody could ask, even with 1,000 or so clams and us three clammers and one spectator aboard.

Then the driveshaft went. A shade tree mechanic looked at it several times, got down on his hands and knees and peered up at the underside, spit a few times, kicked at some oyster shells, studied the sky for a spell and said, "It's gonna run you about a thousand, but I can't say for sure until I get in there, and once I get it running I can't promise you nothing. This here motor weren't built yesterday."

The proprietor of an upscale marine sales and repair shop in Southport didn't even want to hear about it. He referred us to a shop in Leland, 40 miles away.

The proprietor of the Leland shop was very helpful. He sold us a 17-foot Grady White with a 75-hp Chrysler, both about the age of our house, which, as all the neighbors say, is getting on in years.

The Grady White is a serviceable boat and had given us little cause for despair. Then last week, at the dock where we sell clams, my son tried to fire the motor and couldn't get a spark. He turned pale. His wife closed her eyes and assumed a prayerful attitude, and I started trembling.

It turned out to be loose battery connection and took only a second to fix, not costing a dime.

If I run into that old sage from Mort's again, I plan to tell him about it and maybe help restore his soul.

7/17/88

Spirit of Semper Paratus...

US Coast Guard still vigilant

The US Coast Guard, though hurt by budget cuts, outspent and out-manned and often out-maneuvered by drug runners, is still on the job, looking after coastal interests and us dwellers. "Semper paratus," as the hands at the Coast Guard station on Caswell like to say.

Take the other day. We were out on the Elizabeth River, the short leg between the Intracoastal Waterway and the Cape Fear, close to where it empties into the Atlantic, my son and his wife and I, attending to our daily chore, which is clamming.

The river was at dead-low tide and the boat, a 17-foot Grady White, was sitting high and dry atop a shell bank in the middle of the river, about 20 feet or so from the nearest water. To the casual eye the boat might have seemed to be in considerable distress.

My son and his wife were on the far end of the shell bank pea-raking for clams, a process similar in physical demand to hand-hoeing potatoes. Pea-raking on a good day yields necks, the small choice clams that bring nearly three times as much from the wholesaler as the larger chowders.

I was out in the middle of the Elizabeth in knee-deep water scratching for clams. Scratching is a matter of raking the river bottom until you feel a clam buried in the sand or mud or slime — whatever the bottom happens to be at a particular spot — and scooping it up. On an average day the Elizabeth yields, besides clams, some interesting finds — beer bottles, rod and reel, a metal chair, an old shoe.

While we were toiling away, thunderheads began building to the south and west and north. Lightning was flashing beyond Southport and thunder was rolling in from the far yonder.

In the distance over Bald Head Island, down the coast to the west and to the north over the mainland, we could see sheets of rain pouring out of the black clouds scudding across the sky.

Almost anybody would have said it was going to be a rough day. And there we were, still a good couple of hours away from the risen tide, with the boat beached on the shell bank and no easy way out.

Then, down the cut through the marsh to the Coast Guard station, came a rescue boat, making good time until it hit the river. Two Coast Guardsmen were aboard, and in the shallows one of them broke out a pole and began sounding the depths every few feet.

When they got within hollering distance, they asked if we wanted to be rescued. We asked, "From what?" And they said, "Well, you know, the weather." And we said, "What weather?"

Unaccountably, the sun was bathing us in a golden spotlight, with rain and black clouds and thunder and lightning on three sides.

Did we want a tow? My son demurred on grounds that towing the boat from atop the shell bank would tear out the bottom.

Well, did we want the Coast Guard to call anybody for us, maybe next of kin? No. Did we have a radio on board? No, but we did have a flare gun and several shells. We would fire away if things got sticky.

The Coast Guardsmen said they would be watching us with binoculars, just in case. Then they headed back for the cut through the marsh, looking very much concerned.

We resumed our pea-raking and scratching and at high tide boarded the boat and went down to the fish house and unloaded the clams, in bright sunshine all the way. The black clouds and thunder and lightning bypassed us and dumped four inches of rain on Wilmington.

I plan to send a thank-you note to the Coast Guard as soon as I can figure out exactly the right thing to say.

8/7/88

Gull is a 'game' catch...

Down where flying fishes play

At Ocean Isle, in Brunswick County, about 7,000 pounds of spot had been taken the night before. The size of fish catches, like fishermen's chests, tends to swell, but the Ocean Isle report was supposed to be the revealed word.

The spot were taken in nets, which as sport compares with shotgunning guppies in an aquarium. Still, fish are fish.

From the pier at Holden came a report of a 27-pound king mackerel. The king had been seen in the pier house by several whose word could usually be trusted. Telling about the size of a fish is the next best thing to catching it.

From all up and down the southeastern beaches came reports of fish running — blues, Virginia mullet, spot, mackerel, puppy drum, trout, and a few vagrant pompano. You had to be either deaf or bedridden not to get out there and start hauling them in.

For the first couple of hours I got in a lot of good practice casting, polishing my overhand, underhand and sidewinder. The sidewinder requires a deserted beach.

Then there were a couple of hours of practice baiting hooks. I tried shrimp, bloodworms, night-crawlers, cut bait, sand fleas dug from the strand, and an assortment of plugs.

I worked out cunning arrangements of bait — cut bait on one hook and bloodworms, cut bait and sand flea, all on one hook. I nearly bit it myself.

Toward noon, after I had spent nearly four hours getting ready to start hauling them in, an elderly gentleman came out of a cottage and strolled kind of tentatively down to where I was sidewinding. He had a brand new rod and reel. He watched me for a few minutes, seeing how it was done.

His first cast barely made it to the breakers. I could tell he was no fisherman.

On his second cast he hauled in a flounder that must have run between three and four pounds. His daughter came out with a camera and started taking pictures. I inquired politely about what he was using for bait.

The old fellow, whose name got lost in the wind, was a retired postmaster — from Sherrill's Ford, it sounded like. He lived on Lake Norman, near Charlotte. He said the lake had several hundred miles of shoreline —

maybe it was several thousand — and he never once fished it. The last time he had been fishing was 26 years ago, on Cape May, NJ. How was I doing?

Toward mid-afternoon my son came down to the beach, bringing me a folding chair and a sweater. He checked the fish bucket, saw it was empty, and decided not to hang around, sensing a certain lack of joy.

A beach-walker stopped to check the bucket. He looked at me slumped in the chair, nodding in the late afternoon sun, and said, "Catching anything?" I said, yes, pneumonia. He said, "Well, I'll say this for you, you're not risking a heart attack."

The hard strike came about 5 o'clock. The line thrummed like a bowstring and the rod nearly jerked out of my hand. The chair folded and began floating on the tide.

I was all over the beach, heaving and reeling, running into the water and back toward the dunes, wondering where I could locate scales and a photographer. I thought about inviting in the whole neighborhood for a fish supper, with me presiding grandly at the head of the table passing out slices of the monster.

Then I saw the seagull floundering in the waves, beating gamely against the line and practically drowning itself. Ashore, the gull looked at me, somewhat accusingly, I thought, and waited patiently while I cut the line. The gull headed straight south in a bee-line without looking back.

Well, a seagull story was better than no fish story at all. So, getting warmed up to tell it in fine detail, I said to a good friend, "You ever catch a seagull?"

He said, "No, but I caught an albatross once in the South Pacific. We were flying box kites, using thin armature wire for a string, and this albatross ..."

11/11/79

A paen for the old barns...

Obliterating our heritage

The Eastern North Carolina Chamber of Commerce, in one of the fits that occasionally seize uplift groups, is trying to obliterate a part of our heritage.

The chamber wants to destroy the thousands of dilapidated outhouses, tobacco barns and other decaying farm buildings that stand, and in many cases recline, across the Coastal Plains.

The chamber's notion is that the old buildings discourage new businesses scouting about for places to light. A Japanese industrialist touring Eastern North Carolina spots an abandoned house with a sway-backed roof, moss on the north side and kudzu crawling all over, his grin tightens and it's Sayonara.

So, those who own such relics are being asked to donate them to volunteer fire departments for practice in putting out fires, or to dismantle what is left and possibly salvage a good board or a log or two, or maybe take a couple of sticks of dynamite and blow them to smithereens.

In a burst of alliteration, the chamber named the cause "Carolina Clean Countryside Campaign" and described it as a nod to reality rather than putting on airs. Eastern North Carolina's whole agricultural system has changed, a chamber official explained, and all those rotting buildings are relics of an era long gone.

That's so. Those who still cure tobacco more often than not use the mobile metal structures made by Long Manufacturing Co. in Tarboro and leave the old log and tarpaper relics at the edge of the fields to the weeds and weather.

In a corner of Wake County that I regularly commute through, three tobacco barns still stand on a ridge, hard by a country club and an upscale residential development. I figure they are strictly for atmosphere or maybe storing golf carts, certainly not for any agricultural purpose.

In Fuquay-Varina, for a fine example of radical change, tobacco warehouses have been converted into flea markets, indoor used car lots and discount houses, and the babble of shoppers, not the chant of the auctioneer, now carries on the morning air.

Although comparatively few Down Easterners retire these days to an outdoor privy with crescent moon for decor and Sears catalogues for leisure reading and utility, the old outhouses still abound throughout the region, gentle reminders of other times. In recommending their destruction, the chamber of commerce didn't suggest that bodily functions, as well as the agricultural system, had changed, only that the privies were eyesores distracting to those brought up with indoor plumbing.

The chamber of commerce undoubtedly has a point of sorts. Who wants to build condos or a chemical plant or a Hardee's or maybe a nice playland with Putt-Putt Golf and a water slide out in the boondocks with an old tobacco barn or an abandoned farm house or a crazily tilting privy in plain sight, for crying out loud? Nobody, that's who.

Not to challenge the Eastern North Carolina Chamber of Commerce, which certainly knows far better than others what is best for the region, but I am partial to those stretches along 133 and 211 and 421 and 55 where the landscape is marked by old tobacco barns and farmhouses and privies and rusting farm equipment and an occasional general store, permanently closed, with a faded Pepsi sign and boarded windows.

For five years now I have marked the passage of time by the roof-line of an abandoned house in Sampson County, just south of Clinton. In 1982 the roof was merely sway-backed, like a very old mule. Then a couple of years ago I could tell the roof was in terminal condition. Things had started growing up through it. Now the roof is in total collapse, completely fallen in, and only kudzu is holding the outside walls together. You can't mark time that way by the wear and tear on a McDonald's Golden Arch.

My problem is that I am getting as ancient as those old buildings.
10/18/87

Trouble looming in paradise...

The Southport magic

A lot of us who turned to this area for peace and quiet, an uncluttered view of sunrises and sunsets and sailboats beating down the Intracoastal, and a state of mind that puts things in sensible order — fishing first or second, for example — have made a special effort through the years to keep quiet about Southport.

There has been a lot to keep quiet about, some things now long gone but not forgotten.

The thing that first struck me was that many people in Southport, maybe most, just didn't give a damn about many of the things that captivated and energized people elsewhere.

So you find neighborhoods ill-defined: fine homes cheek-to-cheek with little more than fishing shacks, docks and fish houses across the street from historic homes lovingly restored, and in places confusions of commercial and residential development.

A lawn might be manicured and the one next to it cluttered with nets and crab pots and clam rakes and lines and parked in the middle of the whole mess, a boat far grander than the owner's house.

There is still the Robert Ruark mystique about the town, and lately a street has been named for the ill-fated writer. Although Ruark lived in Wilmington, he spent much of his boyhood and young manhood in Southport, hunting and fishing with his grandfather, and he recalled those wondrous days in possibly his finest prose, some of it truthful.

Ruark's summoning the Southport magic could have ruined the town, in the way that Hemingway's novel finally ruined Pamplona. But somehow it didn't, maybe because of that general atmosphere of not giving a particular damn about what Ruark or anybody else thought.

Some of the old landmarks have vanished. The old Frying Pan Lighthouse ship that listed for years in practically the middle of town and served as a bizarre tourist attraction was towed away a few years ago.

But those magnificent oaks, gnarled and ancient, are still all about, giving streets a tunnel-like effect, and the unhurried pace that might strike Charlotteans as excessively lackadaisical is still the standard gear.

There has been trouble in paradise occasionally, scattered signs that different if not harder times were at hand.

A West Virginia Club, peopled by refugees from that benighted state, was formed and began meeting regularly.

Harrelson's grocery, the only family-owned supermarket in town, called it a day and gave full sway to the chains.

The town put in a surrey with a fringe on top, drawn by a spirited white horse, to haul tourists about. Some said that was a touch too precious and might encourage the notion that Southport was trying to become a small Charleston or, worse, a Hilton Head.

A movie company came to town to make a feature film and that threatened to do permanent damage. One of the stars mentioned that

Southport would be a lovely place to settle down in, but nothing came of her chance remark and the town was spared.

Those were minor torments, comparatively speaking. Now comes the cruelest blow of all, one that probably will leave the town beyond hope of recovery or repair.

Rand McNally Retirement Places Rated, a publication that commands nationwide attention among those planning to take the veil, has listed Southport as one of the best places in the country to retire to.

In money matters, climate, personal safety and housing, Southport came out ahead of the top-rated area, a boondocks in Kentucky, and beat the fool out of Myrtle Beach, Hilton Head and West Palm Beach.

By now the madding crowd is probably on the way and there goes the whole confounded neighborhood.

9/20/87

Hunkering down seaside...

Batten hatches for winter

Down here on the coast it amounts to a sea change.

Sandpipers and gulls by the hundreds hunker down along the strand for whatever comfort that gives in the raw wind, and dozens of birds sit along the power lines expropriating a little heat, to the chagrin of Carolina Power & Light, which isn't allowed to charge wildlife.

The birds wheel away from the strand in a cloud, gulls squalling, at the approach of a stroller and then settle again farther down the beach after the presumed danger has passed.

Many of the cottages are battened down now against the winter weather, plastic sheets and plywood covering the windows and doors facing the ocean, shades and blinds drawn.

The town police officer stops to check an open utility room door at a place where no one is supposed to be until next spring. He walks around the cottage, then closes the door and sits on the front deck for a while studying the flat sea.

On the strand at Fort Caswell a volleyball net flaps in the wind. Only yesterday, it seems, throngs of young Baptists down for late-season retreats were all over the area with their boom-boxes, Frisbees and beach balls.

Erosion along scattered stretches of the strand is severe, as it often is this time of year. Bottom steps leading from piers and walkways to the strand that used to be buried in sand now hang in air.

At one of the ocean-front cottages threatened by erosion, new concrete pillars have been poured and cinderblock piled in front — a defensive measure that would appall Orrin Pilkey, the Duke marine geologist who has made a career out of trying to save the NC coast from man's inhumanity to nature.

At other cottages where the dunes are being eaten away, new sand fences have been erected, token signs of resistance.

For most of the beach dwellers there is no need to worry. The ocean's dynamics, which I do not pretend to understand, will bring back the sand in spring and early summer in one of nature's renourishment projects.

A few gill nets are still deployed, one end anchored to the strand and the other reaching out a hundred yards or so with floats marking the far end. The catch this fall has been poor, and it is hard to see why the netters stay at it, particularly in the biting cold. Habit, probably.

The horizon is practically clear of vessels on a Saturday afternoon. A few weeks ago in a late-season fishing tourney, a couple of dozen boats at a time raced out of the Cape Fear and trolled along Caswell in search of king mackerel. Now there is only an occasional container cargo ship headed back to the Orient or an oil tanker returning to the Mideast.

The beach's single public parking lot, where the town elders permit outlanders and upstaters to stop for a glimpse of the ocean and a gambol on the sand, holds a lone pickup truck.

Two women and a toddler bundled heavily against the cold roam the strand in front of the parking lot picking up shells. There aren't many now, no collector's items.

A dead goose is on the strand and the women and toddler give it a wide berth. This area is part of the flyway from Canada south. The goose is still intact, no sign of being shotgunned. Probably just flat gave out.

In another month, after those who came down to celebrate Christmas on the coast have gone and the holiday break for college students has played out, the beach will close down even tighter and those of us who live here year-round once again will peer out the windows at the sound of a car to see what all the commotion is about.

12/11/88

Candidates' controversy...

Gun rack issue is joined

We have here in the Seventh Congressional District the year's hottest campaign issue, not counting White Patriot Party leader Glenn Miller's proposal to fence off the United States from Mexico to keep out illegal aliens and drugs.

At the heart of the issue, popularly known as the Gun Rack Rousement, is the Satellite Syndrome. It all began innocently enough.

Charlie Rose, the sitting congressman, was carrying on in a House subcommittee about a bill he is co-sponsoring to limit scrambling of TV signals carried by satellite — a sore subject in this area.

Out in the pine barrens and live-oak boonies, satellite dishes rank among amenities alongside stoves and refrigerators and indoor plumbing. You can't get a decent TV picture without that dish out in the yard cocked just so.

With a dish you used to be able to pick up HBO and The Movie Channel and all that good stuff free. Then the pay-TV channels started scrambling their pictures so that non-paying dish owners couldn't get anything but wavy lines. That's what Charlie was talking about in the subcommittee meeting.

In the course of the oratory Charlie said, delineating the essential character of your standard Tar Heel rustic, "You have got to own a pickup truck, have a gun rack in the back and a satellite dish on the side of your house." He could also have thrown in the 'coon tail on the radio aerial, the Confederate bumper tag, the little statue of Jesus dangling from the rearview mirror and the cages for the hound dogs in the back of the pickup, but that would have taken up valuable subcommittee time.

Charlie was just speaking gospel truth, of course, being about half good ole boy himself and understanding such things clearly. He has a place at Carolina Beach, which is semi-grit, instead of one of those fashionable layouts on Bald Head Island or Figure Eight or even a condo on trendy Wrightsville Beach, to give you an idea.

The last time I saw him, on a red-eye flight out of Wilmington, he was in shirtsleeves, without a tie, and his shirttail was halfway out, for another good example. Not one to put on airs, he shook about half the hands on the plane, some of them twice.

Charlie had barely gotten gun rack into the subcommittee record when the howl went up. Foremost among the howlers, setting up a regular din, was Tommy Harrelson, the Republican candidate for Charlie's seat.

Tommy is not often identified with the pickup truck crowd. He owns an international gourmet food store that provisions the quality folks on Bald Head and lives in one of those fine old restored houses in Southport's historic district. He wears ties and jackets and blow-dries his hair instead of affecting the greased cockscomb-and-ducktail.

Even so, as unlikely a champion of true grits as he might appear to be, Tommy went straight for the pickup truck vote. "I couldn't believe it," he howled, working up a good head of indignation. "This is the man (meaning good ole Charlie) who should be fighting to help us realize our hopes and dreams and he believes this is all we want to achieve in our lives (meaning a pickup truck with gun rack and a satellite dish out in the yard)."

Strictly speaking, Tommy had a point. A friend who practically lives out of his pickup and is teaching me the folkways of the area said his hopes and dreams include, besides a satellite dish, a double-wide, a stronger motor for his skiff and better nets than the ones he has been using. He would also like some wide-tracks for the pickup. Maybe Charlie will mention those items in his campaign counter-thrust or in his extended remarks in the *Congressional Record*.

So there you have it, Gun Rack Issue tightly joined. It's the first political controversy of the season to really grip the electorate and fire everybody's passion.

5/18/86

Bless those EPA people...

Case against wood stoves

In a rare intrusion into local affairs that deserves warm applause, the federal government in another month or so will begin leaning on wood stoves in the interest of clean air.

The Environmental Protection Agency will propose emission limits for wood stoves similar to the exhaust limits for autos. The proposal is strongly supported by an EPA engineer who said some mornings he can't see the house next door.

In my own case, I can see the house next door every morning and it appears to be on fire from the smoke swirling about. The smoke doesn't bother me, really; some days, especially those when the meter readers make their rounds and missionaries call to save my black soul, I would just as soon for the house to be hidden in a good cloud of smoke.

Neither do I mind the smell particularly. I will take a good whiff of wood smoke any day over the distinctive odor from the Federal Paper Co. that wafts over the area during an inversion. Although Federal is about 20 miles inland, the aroma it gives off can wake people on Oak Island out of a sound sleep. They jerk straight up and holler, "Great God, what is that?"

I don't even mind the chopping, except when it costs me a good late-late TV movie, say one produced in 1935. My next-door neighbor works nights and he likes to split his stove wood around 2 a.m. The chopping produces a metronome effect and lulls me to sleep, sometimes when Jimmy Cagney or Edward G. Robinson is in mid-snarl.

My grievance against wood stoves is deep-seated, going all the way back to my scarred childhood. It has nothing to do with the way my neighbor or anybody else carries on. Live and let live, I always say.

One of my earliest memories is of old granny saying, right after I had gotten out of swaddling clothes, "Run out and gather some kindling, child." When you're trying to build something out of blocks or set up a din with a toy drum, that can be a nuisance.

Later on, when I had gotten some of my growth, it was split wood, bring in a couple of armloads, take out the ashes, build a fire, stoke the fire, blow on the coals, put on another log, knock down the soot, sweep up, do this, do that and the other. It's a wonder I could get any serious reading and hard thinking done.

In the late summers of my pubescent years, my cousins and I, when we should have been playing ball, fishing and reading comic books, were out in the piney woods laying in the winter's supply of stove wood, felling and trimming trees and chain-snaking them behind mules into a clearing where a circular saw jury-rigged to the rear wheel of an old pickup whined them into stove lengths.

In the early autumn of my life, with mouths to feed, bills to pay and a living being pieced together, we depended for heat on a Warm Morning stove, the old-fashioned kind free-standing on a steel mat. I got the wood from right off the homeplace until the owner, who was letting us stay there for insurance purposes, began to complain.

The Warm Morning had a bad habit of belching black smoke at dawn when the door was opened for refueling. Then I would go into my blackface routine to ease the strain.

Now we have a fireplace that has been stone-cold for going on four years. There is oak already cut and split on the back porch and it has been out there for all of three years. I tell everybody I am letting it season. The old woman, who likes a fire for atmosphere, says that excuse is wearing thin.

If the EPA comes through as planned, I can start pleading environmental concern.

12/28/86

Relief from the red tide...

Burst of clamming

We were out on the Elizabeth River, between its fork off the Intracoastal and confluence with the Cape Fear, to celebrate with a burst of clamming the end of the red tide.

It had been nearly three months — or by a shell fisherman's reckoning in pain and suffering, practically a generation — since the red tide shut down clamming and oystering. Those who gather shellfish for a living had gone to seed in a way.

After lying abed mornings for going on three months, it was, to begin with, a real trial to arise once again in the middle of the night, fuel the boat, make it to the ramp for launching and get out onto the water at low tide.

There was also the torment of straining once again muscles gone slack. The basics of clamming — slinging around gunny sacks of clams, manhandling a bull rake and bending over a pea rake — develop groups of muscles that don't come into play for most lines of work, especially not for teaching. After a three-month layoff, the physical misery was almost like starting all over again, so I was told. I didn't sling gunny sacks of clams or manhandle the bull rake or break my back over a pea rake, understand; I was there as an expert observer.

The low tide exposed a ridge in the river that looked like a pile of shells. We anchored there and the clammers got out with their pea rakes, something like ordinary potato diggers, and started hacking and raking. They worked their way along the ridge, coming up with clams now and again and leaving them in little piles. In backbreaking labor, it compared favorably with picking cotton and priming tobacco, both of which I have tried just to see what it was like.

Then they gathered the little piles of clams in a bucket and we were off another shell bank. When the rising tide covered the shell banks, one of them went to the bull rake, a contraption with steel jaws about three feet wide attached to a metal 36-foot handle that can be telescoped down to 12 feet. The long handle enables the clammer to work in water up to 20 feet deep, thereabouts.

The trick is to sling the jaw end out from the boat, while hanging onto the handle, and then drag it along the bottom until it scrapes shells. The clammer then works the handle − looking like someone pumping a railway hand car − hoping to uncover and bring up clams. I tried to sling the bull rake once and nearly ruptured myself picking it up.

While one was handling the bull rake, the other was washing the clams that had been gathered from the shell banks, using a plastic crate to slosh them in the river, and then culling them. They were divided into three groups − cherries, large clams that bring the lowest price; necks, the choice mid-sizers; and seed clams, the small ones that must be thrown back.

After all that hacking and digging, dragging and scraping, washing and culling, they had enough clams to cover maybe the fuel and our sandwiches and soda pops. Ordinarily, with a decent harvest, they would have gone then to the fish house on the Intracoastal and sold the load.

This time it was hardly worth the trouble and it would have been embarrassing to go into the fish house and come out with pin money. So they dumped the load in the shallows and marked the spot by sighting along the bank; they would pick them up on the next trip.

I asked one of them why he did it, toiling that way for a living that might on one of nature's whims, such as the red tide, be cut off, and even in good times be lean.

He chewed that over for a second and then answered, with an explanation that compared nicely with Sir Edmund Hillary's reason for climbing Everest, "It's what I do."

5/30/88

Comparing coast to Orange...

Goodliest land under the cope

The difference between the rolling red clay hills of Orange County, in the Piedmont, and a sandspit in the Atlantic, attached by only a drawbridge to the Coastal Plain, takes some getting used to.

For one thing, there is the smell of salt air delicately scented with the fragrance of fish. After a while the smell disappears, in the same way that the pungent odor of tobacco in summer disappears for those living near Liggett & Myers in Durham.

In the early morning when there is an inversion, or whatever the meteorological phenomenon is that causes it, a musky, brackish odor hangs over the island and clings to the Ocean Highway. That smell compels notice, even from those who have been rooted here as long as the cypress.

The sky seems infinitely larger than it did in Orange County; I am aware that both places share the same one. When a storm is building the sky hangs lower here than there.

Sunrises and sunsets are more vivid – violent slashes of color across the sky. In Chapel Hill, when it is noticed at all, the sunset is glimpsed through trees or between bank buildings.

The cold is colder – a simple matter of humidity that makes 45 degrees here comparable to 35 in Orange County. The wind is stronger than in Orange, although in knots they might be equal.

Residents of the island are hypersensitive to weather, living as they do by leave of the elements. In Chapel Hill a professor looks at a dark sky and says, "It might clear up," and it is a casual comment. Here a fisherman studies black clouds and says, "It might fair off," and it is a profundity. Those who fish only for sport also become sensitized.

After dark, except for the muted roar of the ocean and the crickets' night song, which is still being played in November, there is a vast stillness on the island. A single car on the beach road amounts to a commotion. A light burning on a front porch in the distance is a beacon and a slammed door is a shot in the dark.

In Chapel Hill, before the University went modern and bricked the walkways, and the town, flinging about for something to do, laid side-walks, students and townspeople were readily identifiable, by muddy shoes. Orange County mud, wet, has the consistency of glue and, dry, the staying power of concrete.

Here it is sand. A grenadier who served with Montgomery in North Africa once said the thing that bothered him most in the campaign was not the German tanks or planes or land mines or the infernal heat by day or freezing cold by night; it was the sand — in his food, clothes, cot, eyes, nose, teeth and hair. Every time he reached water he washed himself practically raw.

It is not that bad here. After a rain the sand takes on body and joggers say it gives good footing. Still, those who get about are seldom free of a grain or two.

After a time all these things sink below the level of consciousness. The flora and fauna, the smell and feel and how the weather is become routine parts of existence, routinely accepted, and you never notice them particularly unless you take notes or pause deliberately to ponder.

The thing that dredged them up for me, underlining the radical difference, was a visit to the interior a week ago, the first trip back since moving to the sandspit last summer.

The rolling red clay hills of Orange County seemed like mountains. The heavy fragrance of autumn leaves was downright cloying. The swarms on streets and sidewalks, the frantic pace and crescendo in Chapel Hill took some getting used to.

Even though I had lived there for 20 years, the place seemed foreign. But then, to outsiders, Chapel Hill has always seemed passing strange.

11/18/79

Bemoaning coming ruination...

Year of the coast—or what's left

Out on the causeway just beyond the drawbridge in a semi-wetland is a sign announcing "Coming soon — 18 holes of miniature golf."

A hundred yards or so farther inland on the stretch where, coming beachward, you first glimpse the sparkling Atlantic, is another sign announcing "Future home of Holden Beach water slide." The future is supposed to arrive around the first of May.

There are other signs of the times: "Lots — $119 down" and "This commercial property for lease — will build to suit tenant."

The drawbridge and the Inland Waterway protect the island in the way that drawbridges and moats protected castles in the Middle Ages; this far and no farther.

On the island in these enlightened days of mixed drinks you still can't buy a bottle of Scotch or a drop of wine or a can of beer.

Commercial development is tightly restricted; those for whom hope dies hard say there will be no more — not another square inch.

But there are faint signs that the drawbridge will be stormed and the Waterway forded. There is a quiet but persistent effort to legalize condominiums. An entrepreneur has been reconnoitering the area for a likely spot for a restaurant; it would be the island's first. Everybody says the possibility is highly unlikely. Maybe so.

There is also a persistent effort to get a modern fixed-span bridge to replace or maybe supplement the old one-lane drawbridge. In case the nuclear plant at Southport melted down the evacuation route would be more commodious.

Down the road a piece is Sunset Beach. A few years ago it was a small, largely undiscovered and largely undeveloped sanctuary from urban sprawl. There you could find what is fondly remembered as genteel beach living.

Now the east end of the island has been opened up or, as the word has it, "developed." The east end is as flat and hard as a parking lot, without a trace of vegetation. Standing in the middle of it you seem to be eye-level with the Atlantic. There isn't a dune to obstruct the view.

Four miles south of Sunset is Calabash. If you buy the legend, it used to be a genuine fishing village with natural charm and a magic touch in the kitchen. People came from all over for nothing better than to eat seafood.

They still come to eat, and also to play miniature golf, ride the slides and visit the gift and antique shops. In the neon light you hardly notice the stunning coastal sunset, and there are microwave ovens.

And so it goes, from Currituck to Calabash.

Without half trying you can get an argument either way, sometimes both ways from the same party, on whether North Carolina's seacoast has been hopelessly corrupted.

Jonathan Daniels, the legendary North Carolina newspaper editor long since retired to Hilton Head off the South Carolina coast, was asked a couple of years ago why he had forsaken his native land, supposed to be the goodliest under the cope of heaven. Why hadn't he picked an Eden on the North Carolina coast for his years of reflecting?

With his standard asperity Daniels said the North Carolina coast had been totally bitched. It wasn't his idea of Eden.

Then there is the family on Long Island, in New York, flinging about for months now trying to arrange a permanent move. They see Southeastern North Carolina as a Utopia of sorts, one of the last outposts offering gentility and civility, leisure and relaxation, big sky, calm waters and sweet breezes.

Hope burning bright or nagging despair depends heavily on point of view.

James Dickey, the South Carolina poet, speaking of the planet, might have had it about right for the coast when he said it won't be the atom or even the manswarm that will finally do us in. It will be the bulldozer and chainsaw.

2/10/80

When the boat gets fixed...

Down to sea in ships — or whatever

We have had the boat for about two months now, on loan from the band director across the Waterway.

It is a 15½-foot skiff, hand-built by the band director. The boat is altogether utilitarian. It doesn't even have a catchy name, such as "U-n-Me, Babe" or "The Busted Flush." We call it the boat. (We also call the house the house and the car the car, which, I suppose, puts us in the backwaters of beach culture.)

The boat was accustomed to an outboard motor. We didn't have an outboard. For the first month the boat floated and sat in the canal, depending on the tide, tied to the bulkhead in front of the house.

The band director suggested several times that an outboard would be useful. We looked at several models and backed away, outboards being almost as dear as waterfront property.

The band director suggested oars. We bought a handsome pair, oarlocks and a full complement of lifejackets. Row a 15½-foot skiff against the tide and you get an idea of what the pioneers contended with when they urged prairie schooners across the wide Missouri.

The boat went back to the bulkhead anchorage. It was used mainly by children pretending to fight naval battles. The oars became three-inch guns.

A couple of weeks ago the band director, exasperated by our dilly-dallying, dug out from his belongings an old outboard. It looked like a lawnmower motor set on a drive shaft and propeller. It was supposed to generate up to maybe three horsepower. The pull-cord brought forth several coughs. The band director said to get it fixed and we could have it on loan to go along with the loan of the boat.

The proprietor of the marine supply on the causeway was dubious. He asked what make the outboard was and wrote on the repair slip "motor." He asked what was wrong with it and put down "broke." He stroked a new 20-horsepower job and said, "I can let you have this one for about nine hundred. It lists for thirteen."

A week later the proprietor of the marine supply said, "We were afraid we couldn't get parts in case we needed them. Sure you don't want a new one?"

Ollis Johnson has the outboard now. The barber said to go past Oak Grove Baptist Church and take the unpaved road just beyond the two brick houses. "If anybody in the county can fix it, it's Ollis," he said.

The sand road ended in the middle of an auto graveyard. Ollis was on crutches, his one foot propped on a stump, watching a young man washing out a carburetor with gas. A car motor was hanging from a block and tackle slung over a tree limb.

Johnson must be well into his seventies. He mentioned the touch of rheumatism in his shoulder and arthritis in his hands. It wasn't a complaint, more a matter of taking the morning inventory of what was left.

He peered over his spectacles at the outboard and said, "It must be about as old as I am. What kind is it?" I said I thought it was an early Rolls-Royce. I yanked the pull-cord and got a good baritone cough. He chuckled and said, "It don't matter. I'll have her running in a couple of days. Put it over there inside the shed so nobody will haul it off by mistake."

I have complete confidence in Ollis Johnson. Barring complications, we will be out on the Intracoastal in a few days mingling with the sleek pleasure craft bound for Florida. We might even come up alongside the *Sequoia*, the former presidential yacht now berthed at Myrtle Beach, which occasionally plies our stretch of the Waterway.

I fully expect the band director to be out at the end of his pier clapping and cheering.
11/4/79

V
PEOPLE

The Squire won't say...
– Cold winter? Hugh still hedges

You might be pleased, then again you might be appalled, to know that Duke Power Co. meter readers can make out those little numbers telling how much you are going to get soaked from 15 feet feet away.

Hugh Wilson, the Squire of Bingham Township in Orange County, found this out a few days ago when the meter reader stopped by his place for a reading.

Hugh's dog, who helps her master in every way she can, short of leading him around on a leash, wouldn't let the meter reader get within 15 feet of the meter. So the fellow stood back a way, squinting in the autumn sunlight, and jotted down his findings. Hugh checked the findings, then went over and checked the meter and discovered, by George, that the fellow had hit it head on.

The Squire is knowledgeable about meters, having been during his salad days in the legal department of the Philadelphia Electric Co. He learned then that there were 27 ways to beat a power company meter. He learned last week that keeping a dog on the premises wasn't one of them.

The dog redeemed herself later in the week when a preacher stopped by to check on Hugh's general deportment. After a field inspection, standing out in one of Hugh's pastures, the preacher said in parting, "Want you to come to church Sunday." The dog bit the preacher right in the seat of the cloth.

Hugh said all of this while leading up to a confession that he didn't have a thought in his head about what the weather will be like this winter. He also threw several political observations into his introductory remarks, being chairman of the Democratic Party in Orange County. His general observation was that politics was a little uncoordinated right now. He didn't elaborate and I didn't press him.

I checked with Hugh after reading that forest rangers had noticed an exceptionally heavy fall of mast in the mountains and were predicting another cruel winter for North Carolina. As the acknowledged unofficial long-range winter weather forecaster for this area, Hugh was the obvious one to check with. I haven't taken forest rangers as the last word on anything since one of them mistook an ordinary browning-out for pine beetles in Chatham County several years ago.

Hugh pretty much shrugged off the rangers' forecast. He said fall of mast was nothing but folklore for predicting winter weather and notoriously unreliable. "The acorns around here aren't much to speak of," he said, "and there aren't any persimmons. The holly berries aren't much either. Of course, multiflora rose is loaded." I asked why he had bothered to check if it was nothing but folklore and unreliable, and he said, "It doesn't cost anything to look."

The coats of Hugh's cattle were getting long; one cow in particular was beginning to look downright shaggy. Although the length of the coat was a sound indicator of the kind of winter in store, he wasn't ready to stake his reputation on it.

"The way I see it," he said in his preliminary report, "weather tends to even out. Last winter we had some of the coldest days in a hundred years, so this winter doesn't figure to be as bad. This summer we had all those 100 degree-plus days, so next summer ought not to be as hot. I'm not ready to say that yet, you understand."

He was willing to take a firm stand on snow, even though many of the signs were not ready to be read just yet. "We are due for a good deal of snow this year," he said. "We haven't had much in four or five years, just a few flakes here and there, soft and skimpy, barely enough to leave tracks. We ought to have maybe an eight- or nine-inch fall."

Hugh expects to have his unofficial forecast ready in about two weeks, farm chores and political duties permitting. By then, all the signs ought to be ready, plenty of wood will have been cut for the winter, and he will have finished worrying about the electric bill.

10/2/77

"Skipper" — a semi-reformed editor

"J" School Dean was one of a kind

The journalism school at the University here is looking for a new dean, a matter of orderly change. The sitting dean, Jack Adams, wants to return to the classroom. Nearly 10 years in the job is penance enough.

Chances are the search for a worthy successor will not have as its goal another Skipper Coffin, even if a reasonable facsimile could be found.

Probably that is just as well, the world having turned and times having changed.

For a number of years, beginning in the middle 1920s, O.J. "Skipper" Coffin was, single-handed, what the University euphemistically called its journalism department. Around 1950, the department put on airs and became a school with Skipper Coffin as its first dean. A deanship fit him as naturally as an ascot tie fits a plowhand.

He came to higher education, the teaching end of it, as a semi-reformed newspaper editor. His academic credentials were sketchy. He claimed to have a bachelor's degree in something, without pressing the point.

His idea of an adequate library for the journalism school was a dictionary, a world almanac and the *Bible* (King James Version). At the peak of his deanship the school had an allotment of $50 for books and periodicals, of which $16 was eventually spent.

He recruited faculty members in his standard way, casual. Passing the time with a working newspaperman one day he said, say, why don't you come to Chapel Hill and teach journalism, and the fellow said, why not, and put in more than 30 years at the Skipper's right hand.

The first time I saw Skipper Coffin, with me posing as a student and him posing as a dean, I thought he was possessed. He was striding up and down in front of the desks, puffing furiously on a cigar, wheezing and snorting asthmatically, pale blue eyes bulging, turning fine phrases and cackling at his own earthy wit.

It took only a short while to realize that he wasn't possessed, just nicely oiled.

His style as a teacher was, well, unconventional. He taught editorial writing, for relief from administration, and I had an unbroken string of absences in his class. He cornered me at the end of the quarter and said I owed him about a dozen editorials.

I spent the whole night writing the editorials, bundled them tastefully with a piece of baling twine and tossed them on his desk the next morning. He stared balefully at the bundle, puffing furiously on the cigar, wheezing, eyes bulging, and said if he didn't have to read them he'd give me an A for the course. I said I'd take the A and threw the bundle in his wastebasket.

He did most of his serious student counseling in the Shack, a tumbledown beer parlor on Rosemary Street. His wife called the Shack the Iron Lung, the only place he could breathe with ease and comfort. Those looking for the dean, the ones who knew his ways, checked the Shack first, then maybe his office or his house.

The school never won accreditation, the academic seal of approval, during Skipper Coffin's raucous reign. When one accrediting team came to visit he announced to the members that he was going out for a beer and anyone who wanted to could join him.

In the University's grand scheme of higher education the "J" school probably was an embarrassment. For a fact, academically it had much to be quiet about.

The only things Skipper Coffin had much interest in teaching were respect for the language, belief in the worth of newspaper work, common sense and character. As course offerings listed in a university catalogue those things would look a trifle odd.

The only way for the University to find another one like him — and understandably, it does not seem to be of a mind to — would be to start opening graves.

9/17/78

Young pre-septaugenarians...

Some folks never age

Bill Prouty and Hugh Wilson were killing time in the parking lot of one of the shopping centers in Chapel Hill, each one reminding the other that he was getting along in age.

They must have close to 130 years between them. Bill admits to 63. Hugh won't admit to anything except that he is old enough to vote.

Hugh was wearing a plastic neck collar to keep his head from wobbling. He has had neck trouble since young manhood. The problem dates back to a rowdy night in Louisburg when he was thrown from the rumble seat of a Ford roadster and met a Confederate statue head-on. He insists there was no brain damage, only the neck trouble.

Bill wasn't wearing any visible artificial support. He was wearing wraparound glasses, a helmet, leather boots, Levis, field jacket, and a devil-take-the-hindmost grin. He was sitting on his big Honda and kept revving it up and idling it down, giving the impression that he was anxious to get up with the Hell's Angels.

I have never run across two more unaccountable pre-septuagenarians in my life, not that I have been looking for any.

Prouty waited until fairly late in life, somewhere in his fifties, to take up serious motorcycle riding. The reason for his late blooming is not entirely clear. He is still trying to work some of the restlessness out of his system before risking marriage.

Once he got hooked on motorcycle riding, he threw himself into it, you could say. The first throw was across a Chapel Hill street and into the hospital. Bill cut a turn a trifle thin and joined his foot pedal with a lady's auto bumper. That put him into a cast and on crutches for a while. He said he was thinking about something else at the time.

A couple of years ago, when he was barely 61, he totalled a motorcycle on downtown Franklin Street. He plowed into a line of traffic; the motorcycle stopped abruptly and Bill kept going, describing a graceful arc over a car. He landed on his head and several witnesses said they turned away in horror.

As soon as I heard about the disaster, I called Bill's brother up in Michigan to prepare him for the worst. The next day I heard that Bill was out of the hospital and shopping around for another motorcycle. After that one, a couple of his friends checked to see if they could take out life insurance on him, thinking to turn a quick profit.

To my knowledge, he has ridden a motorcycle up and down both coasts of Florida, without mishap, except once when a car tried to edge him off the St. Petersburg bridge. He has also ridden to northern Michigan and back a couple of times and explored the North Carolina mountains and coastal plains. Taking the wind in his face in good weather has helped to keep his cheeks rosy in his dotage.

When he isn't on the motorcycle he sails, an adventure that he also came to fairly late in life. People standing around the docks at University Lake near Chapel Hill see a boat capsize and watch the skipper in the water clambering to right her and murmur, "That must be old Prouty out there." Usually he sails alone.

Hugh has gotten to be somewhat less adventuresome in the autumn of his life, possibly on account of the neck problem. I understand that he avoids fights whenever possible, unless they deal directly with his honor, and confines his foolhardiness these days mostly to politics, which in some ways can be more dangerous than motorcycle riding and sailing.

Standing there in the parking lot listening to those two old incorrigibles

riding each other about their age, I wondered what had happened to my own sense of youthfulness − not youth itself but the sense of it − and whether in worrying about it I had managed only to lose it.
2/8/76

Lingering letter to Miss Gardner

Dear Ava, if I'd only known

I have been planning for nearly a month now to write Ava Gardner a letter − something along the line of, "If I had but known, dear ..." − since she confessed her true heart's desire.

Ms. Gardner, as you know, is from Grabtown, in Johnston County, a tiny farming community that never had a chance of holding her. For the last 20 years or so she has been a semi-expatriot, working out of London, Paris, Madrid, Rome, the south of France and other places foreign to the Grabtown folks.

Last month in London, on the eve of her 60th birthday, she finally said what I had longed for many years to hear.

The thing she had always wanted, she said, instead of film stardom, international celebrity, the glitter and the gold, was one good man she could love and marry and cook for and make a home for, one who would stick around for the rest of her life.

"I never found him," she said. "If I had, I would have traded in my career in a minute. It meant nothing to me measured against the importance of a marriage that would last."

The bittersweet irony of it all is that I happen to be that man who would have been willing and eager to stick around for the rest of her life while she did the cooking and made a loving home.

I, too, would gladly have given up my career in a heartbeat in exchange for a long and happy marriage − just Ava and me and baby makes three.

I have been in love with Ava Gardner for 40 years; up until now I never thought the time and circumstances were exactly right for saying so.

The tragic part is that she didn't know about my feelings and I didn't have a clue to her true heart's desire, giving our relationship its Romeo and Juliet overtone.

I first realized that I was in love with Ava in 1942, while I was in basic training at Keesler Field in Biloxi, Miss. During a break from close-order drill, a fellow named Stone from Winston-Salem, a graduate of the University here, confided that he had once squired Ava at a dance in Chapel Hill.

"She was about as country as they come," Stone said. "Had nothing to say and blushed every time you looked at her."

Hearing that was like getting hit in the face with a wet squirrel. I stayed away from Stone for the rest of the war.

Through the post-war years I fed my flame mainly in movie houses. I saw *Mogambo*, a truly awful movie, four times, to give you an idea of the depth and intensity of my feelings.

I have seen *The Life and Times of Judge Roy Bean* at least half a dozen times, including television showings. In that one, you recall, Ava is pictured mostly on a poster on a saloon wall. Judge Bean executed a fellow for putting a bullet hole in it, a matter of simple justice.

I still have a hard time accepting Ava's death in *The Snows of Kilimanjaro*.

Our real-life relationship has been what some might call indirect. A few years ago she came back to Johnston County for an Ava Gardner celebration, and my sister, who lives in those parts, told me about it in intimate detail.

I also saw Ava's brother face-to-face a couple of times when he was serving in the NC legislature. I didn't say anything about his sister and me, for fear of breaking his legislative train of thought.

About the letter I am planning to write to Ava — I still haven't decided whether to say anything about Mickey Rooney and Artie Shaw and Frank Sinatra, her former husbands, or whether to mention my wives and nine children.

1/16/83

Remembering John Dunne...

A leader of the movement

Nearly 20 years ago, as the Jim Crow flies, John Dunne was spending his nights and days huddled with three others around the flagpole at Chapel Hill's downtown post office. They were fasting, in another of a long series of protests against racial discrimination in public accommodations.

Chapel Hill then, as now, was longer on its liberal reputation than its liberal deeds.

The fast lasted a couple of weeks or so, as I recall, and the four took only liquids, along with casual abuse and warm praise from passersby. A physician with liberal leanings checked the fasters periodically.

For John Dunne, the trip to the flagpole had been roundabout if not long.

He came to Chapel Hill as a Morehead Scholar, a Yankee in pursuit of the Southern Experience as well as higher education.

When the civil rights convulsion began in Alabama, with Bull Connor turning the police dogs loose and playing fire hoses on the demonstrators, John Dunne went to see for himself. It was in Alabama, so his friends said later, that he was seized by the cause.

On his return to school, a matter of form more than substance, he became, with Pat Cusick and Quentin Baker, a force in Chapel Hill's embryo civil rights movement.

Pat Cusick came to the flagpole by way of Alabama, where one of his grandparents had been a celebrated Klansman. Cusick shed about 30 pounds in the fast at the post office. He was said to be trying to redeem his ancestry.

Quentin Baker, a student at NC Central, had come over from Durham, where the civil rights movement was languishing. In Chapel Hill's civil rights triumvirate, he was the warm-up man, an effervescent spirit who, given the chance, could have had the Merchants Association and Chamber of Commerce singing "We Shall Overcome."

At one of the early rallies, the faithful, slack-jawed and glassy-eyed after being gorged with swollen rhetoric from academics and preachers, were practically comatose. Then Quentin Baker came on and in no time at all had the red corpuscles racing and everybody panting to march.

To those outside the movement, John Dunne was a presence frequently seen but only poorly defined. His sincerity, his deep belief in the cause and total dedication to the movement, were plain enough. But he seemed to consider reporters hired hands of Ross Barnett and George Wallace and kept his distance accordingly.

To those inside the movement, he commanded respect bordering on reverence. You could see it in the eyes of young demonstrators as he taught them how to submit to arrest, by lying inert, and how to handle tear gas, with a wet handkerchief, and the other lessons of passive resistance.

He had about him a certain dignity and grace under pressure that somehow remained intact — once when the wife of a Chapel Hill restaurant owner urinated on demonstrators holding a lie-in, and again when the proprietor of a general store sprayed demonstrators with ammonia.

Efforts were made to strip him of his Morehead Scholarship and of student status altogether, both of which had become literally academic.

In the end Dunne, Baker and Cusick landed in NC prisons. Their sentences were commuted by Gov. Terry Sanford. Dunne went on to Harvard and a law degree at Yale and social service to the young and dispossessed.

Last week John Dunne died, at 39, from cancer, lending weight, perhaps, to Hemingway's idea that the good die young; that the rest of us will die, too, of course, but there will be no particular hurry.
1/9/83

Ended with her usual grace...
A long, happy, useful life

Tending to a death in the family, like figuring income taxes, is vastly more complicated these days than it used to be, even without a lot of sorrowing going on.

The mourners in this case, instead of grieving, were celebrating a long and happy and useful life. The end for Mamie Harness, my wife's aunt, was as serene as much of her life had been. After nearly 93 years, the early ones filled with toil and trouble, she gave up the ghost in her usual graceful way and simply stopped breathing.

She liked ways and things to be neat and orderly, with well-defined beginnings and middles and ends. Fittingly enough, she called it a day on

New Year's Eve, at the end of one thing and the beginning of another.

At the turn of the century, she and her family, plagued by malaria and poverty, came by mule and wagon out of the piney backwoods of Onslow County. They settled in Durham and got purged of the malaria; the poverty hung on through the Great Depression.

Her first job as a teenager, was at the Golden Belt Manufacturing Co., turning out labels and sacks for Bull Durham tobacco. Consistent with her Onslow County upbringing, she stayed at home when it rained. Her supervisor explained gently that Golden Belt's work went on, rain or shine, and that was her introduction to big-city ways.

Soon afterward she gave up what she called "public work" and spent the next 50 years ministering to her ailing parents and tending to brothers and sisters.

Approaching her prime at 65 and shed at last of homebound duties, she finally married and moved to Florida for a long stretch of relative ease and comfort and a new warmth.

For the last two years, in the gentle autumn of her life, she lived with us down here on Oak Island, going through a hurricane and lesser torments with greater serenity than anyone else in the family could summon.

The complications that set in with her death — I realize this is a terrible thing to say at such a time — were almost laughable.

The funeral services were prepaid, as the insurance men say. Unfortunately, the funeral home where the prepayments were made had in the meantime been gutted by fire. Makeshift arrangements had to be fashioned.

Her will and financial affairs were handled by a lawyer in Hillsborough. When a call was made to have the will probated and her affairs concluded, it turned out the lawyer had suffered a stroke and was in a rest home and in no condition to say what to do.

Her best-loved nephew, one who had remained constant and close through the years, was on the West Coast, somewhere between Seattle and San Francisco, and couldn't be notified of her death. Her step-relatives, like other holiday revelers, were out of touch and couldn't be reached until it was too late to attend the funeral.

The funeral director, who, God knows, has troubles enough of his own trying to settle his fire insurance claim, couldn't be found to answer a couple of mindless questions. I left a copy of the obituary with a secretary in an office next door to the funeral home's makeshift quarters.

The obituary clerk at the newspaper in Wilmington looked at me with dark suspicion, as if I were trying to pull a fast one, and never did accept my word that I was merely a messenger bearing sad tidings. That newspaper takes absolutely no chances at all on someone's trying to perpetrate a hoax.

The dark blue suit that I have been saving for solemn occasions turned out to be covered with mold, one of the household hazards of living at the beach.

If Mamie had had any idea of the problems that would arise, she probably would have called the whole thing off.

1/16/85

He can caucus casually...

Kincaid: a minority of one

I have been sitting here for a week now studying the North Carolina election returns and the most unassailable conclusion I have been able to draw is that the Republican minority in the State Senate is going to have an easy time of it holding caucuses next session.

The Republican minority in the Senate for the 1975 legislature will consist of Donald Kincaid of Caldwell. This has definite advantages as well as a few disadvantages.

One possible disadvantage is that Kincaid is going to be the Senate minority leader whether he wants the job or not. He could conceivably refuse to nominate himself, or, in case he did nominate himself, refuse the nomination. But that would leave the Senate minority leaderless and nobody wants to see that happen. So, it looks like this particular honor will be thrust upon him.

In the matter of caucuses, Kincaid will find holding them a snap. Questions as to whether to caucus will amount only to Kincaid's saying to himself, "Well, do I need to caucus on this or not?" Then he will have only to answer himself and proceed accordingly.

Should he decide to caucus, Kincaid will not have to worry about rounding up a quorum, having only himself to get together. The time and place can be of his own choosing. He will be able, for example, to caucus in a telephone booth. The beauty of this arrangement is that he will be able to say at any time and any place, "Sorry, I can't talk to you now. I'm in caucus."

Another definite advantage is that Kincaid will be able to speak for the whole Republican delegation in the Senate without fear of challenge or a whole lot of contentiousness.

Setting Republican policy in the Senate ought to be a fairly simple matter. The only trouble would be if Kincaid happened to be of two minds on some particular matter. Then he would have to say to himself, "Well, now, let's try to get together on this thing."

There would be a minimum of confusion about who speaks for the governor in the Senate and little competition over who will handle the governor's legislation. Unless Kincaid has something to say, it will be fair to conclude that the governor has decided to hold his tongue. When the governor has a pet piece of legislation he wants introduced in the Senate, he might call the minority leader and say, "Kincaid, who do you think ought to handle this? Whom can we trust to put it in the best light and then work for adoption? We need a good party man for this responsibility." And then Kincaid would almost have to say, "Well, governor, going quickly through the delegation, I would say that Kincaid's our man. He's the best party man we've got in the Senate. Of course, if you don't go along with him I'll try to think of somebody else."

A great advantage to reporters covering the Senate is that it will be ridiculously easy to tell when votes are splitting along party lines. When the vote is, say, 49 to 1 and Kincaid is the 1, then it will be safe to report that it split along party lines. It's not all that easy when there is more than one Republican in the Senate.

One of the great disadvantages for Kincaid will be in committee assignments. Lt. Gov. Jim Hunt is a fair-minded presiding officer and chances are he will try to give a bipartisan tone to the Senate committees, within the bounds of political decency, of course — say one Republican member to every 10 or 20 Democrats. If that happens then Kincaid will find himself saddled with membership on every confounded Senate committee.

Weighing one thing against another, the Senate minority will find its work in the 1975 session greatly simplified, much more efficient, and the whole delegation can be expected to speak with a single voice, showing much more unity than it has in years. With all these advantages, it's a wonder the Republicans didn't think of it sooner.

11/17/74

Dressed like an un-made bed...

In remembrance of Al Lowenstein

The first time I saw Al Lowenstein was at the University in Chapel Hill right after World War II. He and I and a couple of hundred others were living in Aycock dormitory, if you could call residence there living.

Aycock was possibly the raunchiest living quarters in Chapel Hill, maybe in the Southeast. The dormitory would make a plate of spaghetti look well organized.

The place was filled with veterans fresh out of service, many fresh out of combat. They devoted most of their dormitory time to Aycock's permanent floating crap and poker games, to tending bar, and to sitting around telling war stories, some of them true. Considerable time was spent devising ingenious ways to avoid classes and study and the dean of men.

And then there was Al Lowenstein. He must have been all of 16 or 17 at the time. He belonged in Aycock, in the midst of that motley collection of free spirits, the way a choir boy belongs in a Chapel Hill fraternity house.

He was fresh out of the Bronx in New York, gangly, apple-cheeked and painfully innocent. His unquenchable enthusiasm, lavished on practically everything, was enough to give the standard Aycock resident a blinding headache.

Physically, Lowenstein gave the impression of a pair of horn-rimmed glasses flying around in perpetual motion on a skinny frame, always in danger of coming apart. The impression was particularly vivid for his Aycock friends and neighbors, who seldom saw anything in sharp focus.

When Lowenstein was really dressed up and carefully groomed, he looked like an unmade bed. To that extent, he fit into Aycock nicely.

He never seemed to study, which would have been a serious breach of etiquette in Aycock. But word spread that he was a brain and he was often pressed into tutorial service by those in danger of being booted off the GI Bill and back into the real world.

I don't think I ever spoke to him, my mind being glazed by higher education in those days. Maybe we nodded in passing.

Fifteen years later, when he was a faculty member at NC State, he became an instant hero in Chapel Hill. Lowenstein was attacked by Jesse Helms, then a commentator for a Raleigh television station, for agitating for civil rights. In those halcyon days, and probably still today, anybody attacked by Jesse Helms for any reason became an instant hero in Chapel Hill.

The last time I saw Lowenstein in the flesh was in the early 1960s, during the civil rights commotion in Chapel Hill. A rally to whip up the spirit among true believers was being held in the First Baptist Church.

Speaker after speaker droned along, nursing the congregation into semi-stupor. The Chapel Hill civil rights movement was in grave danger of failing then and there of its own dead weight.

Then Lowenstein, sitting at the rear of the sanctuary, got to his feet. He was heavier than he had been in his Aycock days. The cheeks were no longer apple-red and the horn-rimmed glasses seemed to blend into, rather than dominate, his general appearance.

In suit and tie he still looked like an unmade bed. The burning intensity was still there, mostly in his voice and eyes.

I've forgotten what he said, but I remember clearly how he said it, with that thousand-yard look in his eyes, and its effect.

The congregation came alive. They marched out of the church and around the corner and held a spontaneous demonstration in front of a drug store that refused to let blacks sit in the booths.

That was the last time I saw Al Lowenstein in action.

His death, being gunned down in his Manhattan law office, was probably in keeping with today's general reign of terror around the world.

It will still take a long hard time accepting that he is gone.
3/23/80

MacNelly's 'P. Martin'...

Shumaker: inspiration for 'Shoe'

This has been a crowded week for me, being an instant celebrity and all.

A publisher once told me, in my newspaper days, "You belong on the comic page instead of the editorial page." And that is where I have finally landed, it seems, after all the years of striving, thinly disguised as Purple Martin Shoemaker. (The publisher, incidentally, now writes his own editorials, and I wish him well.)

I owe the instant celebrity to Jeff MacNelly, who, it turns out, lacks proper respect for his elders. In our days together on the old *Chapel Hill Weekly*, when he was doing the editorial page cartoons and I was unwittingly creating the prototype for P. Martin Shoemaker, I had taken MacNelly for a regular enough young man, if a trifle loose-jointed. He was the only one I've ever seen who appeared to be sprawling all over the place while standing up straight.

I still have right much regard for him, even though he won the Pulitzer Prize at the disgusting age of 24. He said at the time that the Pulitzer judges had to be out of their minds and I readily agreed. (This was not said out of envy or any sense of injustice. Having been passed over for 30 years running, I know better than most how unstable the Pulitzer panel is.)

Anyway, MacNelly's comic strip, entitled "Shoe," began running last Monday in *The Observer* and about 249 other papers. I had been given plenty of warning by Joe Doster, who used to be a reporter for *The Observer* and now is Managing Editor of the *Winston-Salem Journal*. Joe sent me some advance copies of the comic strip along with a note saying,

©Tribune Media Services
SHUMAKER PUTS ANOTHER EDITION TO BED...

"It's you, Shu, it's you." I figured Joe had been working too hard and needed a rest.

Then, last Monday night, when I got home from standing around in the post office, there was a good friend waiting on the door stoop, clutching the comic page in his hand. He wanted me to autograph the confounded thing. I did, signing it, "Jeff MacNelly, Pulitzer Prize Winner."

A former colleague telephoned to ask if I still had the ragged tennis shoes that I always wore to work at the old *Weekly*. She wanted to have them bronzed, for crying out loud. I didn't have the tennis shoes. I contributed them to the Thrift Shop, taking a tax deduction, and the Thrift Shop threw them out.

Several stopped me on the street to ask if I was really P. Martin Shoemaker and I denied it hotly. I have never in my life used a trash can for a desk – orange crates, yes; trash cans, no.

Then a graduate student at the University said she had seen MacNelly on network television, the *Today* show, and he had identified me as the inspiration for P. Martin Shoemaker. I told her you couldn't believe anything nowadays unless you read it in the newspaper.

To seal me up tight, an editorial writer for the *Greensboro Daily News* who, I take it, was having a terrible time trying to come up with something fit to print, said I was the real-life P. Martin Shoemaker. I am about halfway through composing a letter to the Editor of the *Daily News*.

My sister who is married and lives in Tarboro called and asked if I would take it personally if she dropped entirely her maiden name. She is a proper lady and has nice friends and good standing in the community. I listened to her whine for several minutes and told her she must have dialed the wrong number.

My oldest daughter looks at me these days, laughs and says, "Want me to get your sneakers for you, P.M.?" In a way, I find that satisfying; I had never known her to read anything for the last few years except the telephone memo pad to see who had called.

A Baptist preacher sent me a note saying, "Did you really tell people to stick it in their kazoo?" I have to thank MacNelly for cleaning up my language, if nothing else.

There is a card table outside the post office this week, where names are being gathered on petitions protesting curbside garbage collection in Chapel Hill. I said what the heck, why fight it, and signed, "P. Martin Shoemaker."

9/18/77

Billy Arthur is authority...

What a navel career!

Billy Arthur, the Charlotte native, used to be a vaudevillian, a newspaper publisher, member of the legislature, and reading clerk of the NC House of Representatives. He was also for many years, before going into semi-retirement, North Carolina's foremost authority on belly buttons.

In his career as a belly button expert, he conducted a census each summer at White Lake, in Bladen County. Billy is about 38 inches tall, which puts him at eye-level to most belly buttons. His altitude made the White Lake census a fairly simple matter.

The Arthur census, generally regarded as definitive, was of the "innies" and "outties." The innies were those whose belly buttons went in, like the navel on the Pillsbury doughboy; the outties were those whose belly buttons stuck out.

After doing the empirical research in the summer, Billy spent part of each fall writing extensively on the subject, explicating the count. The annual Bill Arthur Belly Button Census Report was accepted by belly button watchers as authoritative, much in the way the decennial US Census is accepted by the public today.

After checking his files a couple of days ago, poring over long lists of innies and outties, Arthur said, no, he had never observed a single off-center belly button in all of his summers at White Lake. The idea of a belly button on the bias seemed to violate his sense of aesthetics.

"I've seen belly buttons hidden in rolls of fat," he said. "No, wait a minute. I couldn't have seen them if they were hidden in fat. I guess I just figured they were in there somewhere. Those didn't count in the census. If I had seen one off-center I would have taken a picture of it and made anthropological history."

Well, as an expert, did he think $854,219 was fair compensation for a woman whose belly button had been moved two inches off center by a plastic surgeon? (You will recall that Virginia O'Hare, an otherwise attractive 42-year-old, was awarded that sum by a New York jury. The plastic surgeon performed a "tummy tuck" to give Mrs. O'Hare a nice flat belly and, in addition, relocated her belly button to one side. Mrs. O'Hare said she was shamed and disgraced by the result.)

"I never knew you could give a 42-year-old woman a flat belly with plastic surgery," Arthur said. "I know a couple I ought to recommend it to."

"What about the $854,219? Was that a fair price?"

"You got to remember," Arthur said, "that women set a lot of store by their belly buttons. They're very close to them, you know. When I was in vaudeville I knew one who wore a rhinestone in hers. If her belly button had been set off to one side I expect she would have worn an overcoat all the time, or maybe a girdle.

"On some women the belly button can be a real beauty mark, a thing to behold. On others, of course, that wouldn't be the case. It's like dimples, cute on some, just an anchor for the fat on others. I would say $800,000 or so would be an absolute minimum for some of the belly buttons I've seen. In Mrs. O'Hare's case, I can't say. It would depend on how her belly button looked before."

I asked him if he would be satisfied with $854,219 in damages if somebody moved his belly button two inches off-center.

"Son," Arthur said, "for that kind of money they could put mine in the small of my back. They could put it on my shoulder. They could put it...."

At that point, Bob Quincy, the sports columnist, walked in, interrupting Arthur's inventory of his body parts. He picked up on the conversation right away.

"When I was in Alaska during the war," Quincy said, "I ran into this girl and she didn't have a belly button at all."

8/13/78

He seemed faintly amused...

A memory of Billy Graham

Billy Graham and I go back a long way, although I am probably the only one who clings to the memory.

We go back 37 years, to Columbia, where in the spring of 1950 he conducted the original crusade that he reprised this past week in a condensed and more modern version.

He came that first time into Columbia from Los Angeles, where he had made headlines by persuading a notorious underworld figure and several celebrities to commit themselves to Christ. As a young reporter on top of current events, I had never heard of him, naturally.

The first time I saw Graham was at a press luncheon in the old Wade Hampton Hotel. In standard newspaper reporter style I spent the early part of the luncheon eating everything within reach.

When I finally looked up from the plate, there stood Graham, surprisingly tall, blond hair shining, deep-set eyes a-glitter, and with a smile that seemed faintly amused. Reporters eating a free meal are often an amusing sight.

He didn't touch a bite, even though the food was first-rate.

Graham wouldn't have had a chance to eat anyway. He talked through the whole meal and was still going strong when I eased out of the room to get on back to work. The reason for my going to the press luncheon in the first place was to get a free meal, not to take notes and all that.

Later on I had a private interview with Graham in his suite in the Wade Hampton and discovered him to be the most unusual preacher in my experience. He rehearsed for his appearances — voice, hand gestures — and didn't mind saying so.

He also confessed a passion for golf and had a set of clubs in a corner, right out there in plain sight. The Baptist preachers I grew up with would as soon have been caught in the pool hall on Saturday night as on the golf course, for crying out loud.

Graham guided the interview, since I wasn't full of sensible questions, and at the end gave me a copy of one of his books, *Calling Youth To Christ*. I still have the book somewhere and plan to ask him to write something personal in it if we meet again.

The Columbia crusade ran for three full weeks, I believe. The nightly meetings were held in a municipal building, the name of which I can't recall, a drafty old barn with a stage across which Graham strode, back and forth. Only the windup on a Sunday afternoon was held in the football stadium. As a member of the working press, I always had a choice seat even when I wasn't exactly working.

Graham threw me into mild shock with his very first sermon. He used as his text something from *Life* magazine, furling the magazine and waving it about and thundering. At one point he pointed to his daughters sitting with their mother in the first row and said he had rather see those two little golden-haired girls dead than living under Godless communism. That got my attention.

He got the attention also of the politicians in the state, practically every one of whom tried to stand at Graham's side, especially when newspaper photographers were shooting. This was when television was in its infancy and unable to handle such events.

At one memorable gathering, Jimmy Byrnes, the Secretary of State under Roosevelt, later to become Governor, got to Graham's side on the stage and announced to the congregation, "I have stood with presidents and kings, but this is the proudest moment in my life."

Burnett Maybank, the US senator from Charleston, also had something to say, but hardly anybody could figure out what it was, his talking Gullah about half the time.

I appreciate the memory and a fairly reasonable excuse to recall it.
5/3/87

Beats the bottle, he says...
Whittler cuts a new life

I don't mean to jar anybody's idea of the bucolic life, but in my years in Chatham County I have run into only one genuine whittler.

I know, the popular notion of life in the sticks is one of wise old souls sitting about pot-bellied stoves or on soda pop crates or hunkered down on their heels, squirting tobacco juice, philosophizing laconically, and whittling small masterpieces. Norman Rockwell did a lot to ingrain that notion with his *Saturday Evening Post* covers.

For a fact, there are a lot of them, not necessarily wise, sitting around down here, next to pot-bellied stoves, on soft drink boxes, anywhere they can find room to take the load off their feet. A good many also squirt tobacco juice, right at your shoes if you get pushy. And some are philosophers, if you count praising George Wallace as laconic philosophizing.

But whittlers, no. Oh, some of them will hack away at a piece of soft white pine, mainly to fill in those stretches when they can't think of anything to say or are so furious they won't risk speech. But the result is generally the reduction of a fair-size block of wood to a toothpick, and I don't call that whittling.

The one genuine whittler of my acquaintance is not even what you would call a rustic, strictly speaking, although he often affects that role. He owns and operates a gas station-grocery-hardware store complex on the Pittsboro highway about three miles from our place. He wears bib overalls at work and his jaw is always bulging with a healthy chaw. That's mostly to make his regular trade feel comfortable and to disarm the Chapel Hill transients. By background and training, he is a city boy and he is about as bucolic business-wise as NC National Bank.

He got into whittling as a way of getting off the bottle, using it in much the same manner as others use Alcoholics Anonymous. The way he tells it, he came to early one morning several years back to find himself trying to fly a kite from a cupola on top of the old Ocean Forest Hotel in Myrtle Beach. That experience suggested to him that it might be time to give up hard drink, and so he did.

In his drying-out days when he felt the old need beginning to come on, instead of calling Alcoholics Anonymous he would pick up a piece of wood, haul out his pocketknife and begin whittling. That took his mind off hard drink and also helped to steady his hands. It didn't hurt his business any, either; some would hang around to see what he was carving, buying soft drinks, peanuts and the like in the meantime.

The whittling didn't take care of the whole problem. He had to get used to a new set of friends and learn to slide away from the old ones. He had to become accustomed to looking at the world, his part of it, clearly instead of through an alcoholic haze. He had to take on a different idea of life itself. Whittling gave him the handle to work the change.

His early work wasn't overly ambitious. He whittled slingshot handles, baked them in an oven and handed them out to youngsters in the neighborhood. They were good slingshot handles but not what you would call truly distinguished carvings.

Then he started turning out swords patterned after the ones the Roman gladiators used and distributed those to the young. Next came wooden chains and necklaces and bracelets. If you think those are easy to make, try it sometime.

I was particularly struck by a ball in a cage and couldn't figure out for the life of me how he had carved it. He didn't say, just smiled with the pride of whittlership.

The last time I was in his place, a week or so ago, he was studying the grain of a piece of wood and tracing a delicate outline that looked like a fine filigree. I asked him what it was going to be. Without looking up he said, "This here's gonna be one of them air thangs you set hot bowls on." He talks that way when he's in character; actually his English is just as good as yours and mine.

Without his UNC class ring, digital wrist watch, foreign sports car, and maybe if his hair was a good deal grayer, he would make a fine model for Norman Rockwell.

6/1/75

She had a special knack...

The art of maintaining order

Annie Swindell began her teaching career in a country school more than 60 years ago, long before anybody thought to ask the White House and Justice Department for help in putting down unruly behavior.

On her first day at school, the students tied her in a chair and dangled her from a second-floor window. She sat out there, twisting slowly in the wind, until the principal ordered the students to haul her back into the classroom.

Unbound, and surprisingly unruffled, she told the principal she could take it from there. The principal left and she proceeded with the lesson for the day, as though nothing untoward had happened.

Years later when she was teaching in Durham High School and young louts became restive, Mrs. Swindell would tell that story about her first day at the country school. The message she got across was that we couldn't do anything she hadn't already handled. The story had a remarkably settling effect.

James Wadsworth, one of Mrs. Swindell's fellow teachers at Durham High, took a more direct approach to unruly behavior. In addition to teaching, Wadsworth coached boxing, and in his prime was about the size of Larry Holmes and had a similar disposition.

For semi-unruly behavior, he would pinch a blood blister on you. Downright unruly behavior brought sterner measures.

A halfback on the football team, a large and rough fellow himself, made the mistake in a thoughtless moment of cursing Wadsworth. Wadsworth laid him out, stone-cold, right there in the high school corridor, with a brisk right to the jaw.

If a teacher did that today, he and the principal and the school board and maybe the State Board of Education would face criminal and civil lawsuits and widespread opprobrium. There wasn't a ripple then, except among the students; they looked at Wadsworth sideways and gave him a wide berth.

By far the best I ever saw in putting down unruly behavior was in the principal at the old Murphy School in northern Orange County. In the 1930s, before it became a night club, Murphy was a one-room schoolhouse, grades 1-6, first-graders in one corner, second-graders in another, and so on. Two grades played outside while the others were being taught.

In those close quarters unruly behavior could not be tolerated if teaching and learning were to occur. The problem was aggravated by the size of some of the students. Although they were fifth-and sixth-graders scholastically, several students were almost drinking age, raw-boned, and ran to about 190 pounds and 6-foot-2.

The principal was a wizened little fellow who couldn't have lifted his weight with the help of the other faculty member. But he made up for his lack of size with a cold stare and an acid tongue.

Strapping farm boys who could toss him like a bale of hay would, under that black stare and tongue-lashing, blanch and then bend over, grab their ankles and await their licks from the paddle.

Whether it was the discipline or something in the well water, they learned to read, write, spell and do arithmetic and to know the general location of the Tigris and Euphrates rivers.

Annie Swindell and the old Murphy principal are long gone, from school and this world. It is probably just as well. They wouldn't know how to act now, professionally anyway.

1/15/84

Reviving an old custom...

Take home a free plant

The arrested alcoholic who built a gas station-grocery-hardware store empire on 15-501 in Chatham County has turned from wood-carving to the care and feeding of plants.

When he forswore the bottle some years ago he turned to wood-carving to take his mind off drink and to steady his hands. After a while he got so good at it, turning out minor works of art, that his avocation threatened to overshadow his vocation.

With all the praise the public showered on him for his carvings and the fascination his work held for children, of whom he is fond, it appeared that wood-carving would become a permanent part of his life. As it is with all arrested alcoholics, there was always the chance that he would backslide and his carving would suffer. But I never thought that plants would be the thing to do it.

The first hint I got that something was afoot was when I drove by his homeplace a while back. A couple of hundred potted plants were lined up beside the house with the lawn sprinkler turned on them. I didn't think much of it at the time, figuring that somebody in there was just crazy about plants.

The next hint I got that things were not altogether the same was when I went into his hardware store for a sparkplug wrench. There were potted plants all over the place. Some of the regular merchandise had been pushed aside to make room for plants. I didn't pause at that either. He is a canny businessman and I figured that maybe he had detected a developing plant shortage.

As it turned out, the plants at the side of the house and in the hardware store were only the tip of the iceberg. His wife said the inside of their house was the worst of all. It was hard to find a place to sit down anymore. There were plants in the bathrooms and bedrooms and she couldn't find anything in the kitchen because everything had been moved to make room for sprays and plant food. She didn't know whether to laugh or cry.

I asked her where the former wood-carver might be found, and she said he was at home, building a greenhouse in the backyard. "From the framing," she said, "it looks like it's going to be bigger than the house."

I finally got up with him last weekend in the grocery. Incidentally, his car has a new bumper sticker saying, "Save The Hydrangea." He was walking around with a can watering plants.

I asked him if he had lost his mind, turning his home and business into a potted greenbelt. He finished watering the plants and stored the can before settling down to answer.

"You know," he said, "when I was a kid we never let anybody get away from our house without giving them something. Piece of ham, pie, quarter of a cake, bread if my mother had just baked. Maybe it wasn't much, but we always gave callers something.

"It wasn't just us. Everybody did it. Everybody I know, anyway. Every time we went to see somebody they always gave us something to bring home.

"I got to thinking what a nice custom that was and why nobody did it anymore. So I decided to start it up again, one way or another.

"I couldn't give away food, naturally, since I'm in the business of selling it. It wouldn't be good business to give away anything we've got for sale here.

"I considered giving a woodcarving to everybody who came, but I saw right off that I wouldn't be able to keep up with the traffic. I finally settled on plants. That's what they're for, to give away."

I mentioned that from the size of his inventory he must be expecting everybody in the county to come calling. He said, "Well, you know how it is. Word gets around and pretty soon people stop and say hello and stand there waiting for their plant. I don't care. Everybody who comes as a friend will get one."

I had my doubts that he would be able to revive the old custom single-handedly, the times and people having changed. These days, you try to press a pan of biscuits on some callers and they would figure you were slightly touched.

He said he didn't care about that either, and which one would I like. I selected a wandering jew for the kitchen window.

8/6/75

That day back in '48...
Pete Seeger ducked eggs

It was a few days ago, and Pete Seeger, the troubadour who spends most of his energy these days trying to clean up the rivers and streams of America, was paddling down the Cape Fear, near Fayetteville.

According to the account I read, he was wearing a flowered shirt, unbuttoned to the warm Carolina sun, and a full beard befitting an aging folksinger. Now and again he would rest the paddle, relax and sing snatches of river tunes.

Nobody was throwing tomatoes or bottles or rotten eggs or trying to break a chair over his head. The change must have come as a relief.

The first time I saw Pete Seeger, the only time in the flesh, was in 1948, in Durham, when he was hiking the presidential campaign trail with Henry Wallace, warming up the audiences with his banjo, and a repertoire of workers' songs and some he made up himself, on the spot.

The Progressive Party was holding its state convention in the old armory in Durham, and it brought out the strangest assortment ever congregated for a political function, before or since. There were confessed and closet Communists from Duke and the University in Chapel Hill and flaming young liberals who wanted to save the world, but were not yet quite ready to give up the checks from home for the cause. There was also a sizable delegation from Durham's redneck element to see that regional and national honor wasn't trampled. I was there as an expert observer.

In the afternoon session, Mary Price of Greensboro graciously accepted the Progressive Party nomination for Governor. A UNC law student consented to run for Lieutenant Governor, and a young fellow who seemed to have wandered onto the stage by mistake agreed to run for Attorney General. All nominations were by acclamation, with a minimum of parliamentary procedure.

During the proceedings, Pete Seeger, a wraith-like figure in those days, wandered about, hitting his banjo a lick when the roar went up for somebody's nomination.

The high point of the convention came that night when Henry Wallace himself arrived to exhort the faithful. The introducer pointed to the main entrance and told everybody to watch for Wallace to materialize. While everybody was looking that way, Wallace burst in through a side door surrounded by a flying wedge of friends and protectors and was hustled onto the stage.

That was when the delegation from Durham's redneck element gave him a little taste of Southern hospitality. Wallace had no more than opened his mouth to say whatever it was he had in mind when the tomatoes and eggs started flying.

As an expert observer, I stood on a table for a good view of the action and it was the doggonedest sight I have ever seen at a political gathering. There was Wallace with his cowlick down on his forehead pounding the lectern and shouting, "I will not be intimidated," and eggs flying past him by the dozen, tomatoes by the peck.

I saw a metal chair go up and come down on the head of a member from the redneck delegation and the fellow crumpled like a rag doll. I thought he was dead for sure. Later on he shook his head and got back into the fray. His moment of truth made a full-page picture in *Life* magazine.

Standing there on top of the table observing expertly with eggs, tomatoes and an occasional bottle whizzing by, it suddenly dawned on me that the other expert observers were underneath the table. So I got under there with them to compare notes.

The last glimpse I had of Pete Seeger, he was pushing his way through the mob, holding his banjo up high with both hands trying to keep it out of the crush. Paddling a canoe down the Cape Fear under the warm Carolina sun is a good deal more idyllic.

11/23/75

Can candidates pass these tests?...

Toward a more colorful stump

Jim Gardner, the Republican candidate for Lieutenant Governor, has created an exciting new dimension in NC politics and at the same time restored to the stump some of the color that had been sadly lacking for, lo, these many years.

The new dimension is the candidate's drug test. Gardner had himself tested to show the people that he isn't stoned out of his gourd, and to show state employees and would-be state employees the way to truth and light.

Now, besides challenging each other to debates, candidates can be expected to challenge each other to drug tests, and maybe, if the idea catches fire, to AIDS tests, Breathalyzer tests, polygraph and Rorschach tests. Many voters would be comforted to know that candidates for exalted office were not only drug-free but AIDS-free, sober, honest and fairly sane. Nowadays, it's often hard to tell whether a candidate is all there, whether he's tripping or hallucinating or simply lying. Professionally certified tests would help to erase those nagging doubts.

Besides the public service such tests offer, it is downright exciting for a candidate to take to the stump, as Gardner has been doing lately, and holler something like: "I passed my drug test. I'm talking CLEAN. No other candidate can make that statement."

The only thing to compare with it for campaign color and thrills came in 1984 when Rufus Edmisten, a Democratic candidate for Governor, fiddled and nasal-twanged mountain folk songs, and Eddie Knox, another Democratic candidate for governor, sang some wonderful gospel hymns, including "Amazing Grace."

Gardner, with his drug test, is in a fine old NC political tradition that goes back at least half a century.

In the 1930s, Gov. Clyde R. Hoey, later to become a US Senator, didn't undergo a drug test, possibly because it would have puzzled voters of the time. But he did wear day-in and day-out a swallow-tail coat, wing-tip collar and red carnation, an outfit that made a lot of people look at him sideways.

Another Governor who went on to become a US senator, Kerr Scott, had as the centerpiece of his senatorial campaign a "calf walk." The point of the calf walk never was crystal clear, unless you counted the calf droppings as somehow symbolic, but Scott managed to get rid of several culls from his Haw River dairy herd.

Gov. Luther Hodges' most memorable piece of political theater was his taking a shower in his undies to plug NC textiles. A picture of the shower scene made *Life* magazine and was often compared favorably with the *Life* picture of Strom Thurmond standing on his head on the lawn of the SC Governor's mansion.

Musically inclined candidates, besides Edmisten and Knox, included Ray (Our Ray) Stansbury, a long-ago candidate for Lieutenant Governor, and David McKnight, a pretender to the US Senate.

Our Ray wore bib overalls on the campaign trail and sang and picked banjo. In the late stages of the campaign, when his election seemed to be in grave doubt, he did most of his singing and picking in Chapel Hill fraternity houses.

David McKnight ran for the US Senate after falling victim to the editorial writer's dread occupational hazard. While explaining daily in editorials for a Fayetteville newspaper how to balance the federal budget, calm the Mideast and settle numerous other cosmic issues, he figured his proper place was in Washington, not in a grubby cubbyhole on Hay Street. So he took to the hustings, fiddling a happy tune, literally.

Possibly the most electrifying moment in an NC campaign in modern times came about 15 years ago, when a Greensboro car dealer, a candidate for high office, Lieutenant Governor or some such, in his first appearance on the stump, this one on statewide television, seized the occasion to quit the race then and there.

It could conceivably happen again, especially with a candidate who flunks his drug test.

8/28/88

For 'Dr. Raney'...

Medicine came first, then letters

I never met Dr. Raney Stanford in the flesh. He died last week, so now I never will.

His son, Raney Jr., and I grew up together, loosely speaking. We were in the same grades in junior and senior high in Durham. In college after World War II we saw each other occasionally in passing, little more than nodding acquaintances by then, the way casual friendships often go, given a test of time.

Raney Jr. gave medicine a wide berth, to Dr. Stanford's deep but unspoken disappointment, I learned later. He did go on to graduate studies and eventually became a college professor. That was solace of a sort, although not a satisfactory substitute for medicine. To Dr. Stanford there was no satisfactory substitute for medicine.

Raney Jr. was living in California when his father died, so the newspaper obituary said. I happened upon the obituary by chance. The notice was just a couple of inches of type without a headline, buried in a half-page of deaths and funerals. You would never have known from reading it that he had been a great diagnostician, or anything other than a physician.

I wondered about Raney Jr. for a second, where he had finally landed and how his life had been. But I thought mostly about Dr. Stanford, whom I had never met and still knew far better than the son.

Our relationship, the doctor's and mine, lasted for several years and consisted entirely of communication by letter and telephone. During that time I was with a weekly newspaper in Chapel Hill and Dr. Stanford, well into his seventies then, was still going to his office in Durham but apparently doing little other than composing letters to the editor.

Every couple of weeks or so he would telephone and get right to the business at hand, saying, "I want you to listen to this before I put it in the mail." Then he would read the letter, from Dear Editor down to yours truly, sometimes backing up to rewrite as he went along. Often he would read particularly good passages twice so I would appreciate fully what would be coming in the mail. After the reading he would explain in considerable detail the burden of the message, to make sure I got the significance of the letter.

Occasionally he would be inspired again after calling and add to the letter or make substantial changes in the original version, in which case he would call and read the whole thing to me again.

Toward the end of our correspondence when his strength was ebbing, he had his secretary do the reading over the phone. Dr. Stanford would listen in on an extension, breaking in to make editorial changes and offer helpful asides. He never had much confidence in this arrangement, even though the secretary seemed to me to be an exceptionally fine reader. He would always call a couple of days after the letter had been mailed to make certain it had arrived in good order.

Dr. Stanford's interests, as expressed in the letters, were broad and deep. One of his great letter-writing campaigns was for the protection of quail. Hunters were decimating the quail population, as he saw it, and he wanted the state to create quail preserves such as those maintained for other wildlife. I don't know whether anybody paid attention to his periodic appeals, except for him and me and the secretary.

Sometimes in idle conversation, after the letter-to-the-editor business had been attended to, he would talk about what Raney Jr. was up to at the moment, about the Durham of 30 and 40 years ago that I could barely remember, and once in a great while about himself and how he was getting along.

At the end of practically every call he would invite me to visit him at his office in Durham. We could put our feet up and solve the world's pressing problems. I always accepted the invitation and said I would be over one of these days.

I never went. Now, far too late, I wish I had.

1/28/79

In praise of mothers' messiah...

Dr. Spock: only his patients aged

Let us now praise Dr. Benjamin Spock, the messiah to mothers (ret.), founding father of the permissive society, corrupter of the nation's young, practicing rabble-rouser, jailbird.

He came loping into Chapel Hill last weekend to rouse the young and praise the sun. He was only a week out of jail in Seabrook, NH, where he had been arrested for demonstrating with the Clamshell Alliance against a nuclear power plant. A matter of polishing his credentials, you might say.

His North Carolina appearance, in Chapel Hill, showed that his sense of direction was still good — uncanny for a 75-year-old retired pediatrician. If there is a place in North Carolina where youth still burns with a hard gem-like flame, a doubtful possibility at best, it is probably Chapel Hill. Besides this state's most appropriate place, he had an appropriate sponsor, the University's Curriculum in Peace, War and Defense, all three of whose component parts Dr. Spock has demonstrated for or against.

Some remembered Dr. Spock best as the author of *Baby and Child Care*, the once-celebrated best-seller lately condemned as the genesis of the permissive society. Being neither young nor rouse-able, they didn't go hear his rousements; they simply muttered querulously at his coming.

Others, the old firebrands from the protest movements of the 1960s, cooled and graying these days, remembered Dr. Spock as one of their own, the father figure protesting nuclear arms, lying in the streets for civil rights, going to jail during the celebrated March on Washington in protest of the war in Vietnam. Few of the old firebrands went to hear Dr. Spock's rousements either. Mostly they expressed astonishment at the appearance in the flesh of a ghost from the past. (The flesh alone was disconcerting enough: coatless, overall mod, and accompanied by a child bride, comparatively speaking.)

The young people Dr. Spock had come to rouse turned out to be not exactly rabble. They were largely from North Carolina's great middle class, the get of mountain, Piedmont and coastal plains respectability. He had met them many times before, at colleges and universities as he campus-hopped back and forth across the land.

Today's students, unlike those of the 1960s, were uniformly practical, sober-sided, cautious, concerned mainly with themselves and their careers. They did not take to changes that might cost them campus life, jobs or public approval. The political activists of yesteryear were nowhere to be found.

The first time he was jailed, he recalled, he came hard up against the realization that American justice was tempered by money. Those with it got off with slight discomfort; those without it felt the full and often angry force of the law. The realization relieved him of his awe of authority and left him, at the ripe age of 60-something, a liberated man.

Dr. Spock, recommended that everyone, especially those students from the great middle class, get arrested at least once for an honorable cause. The cause might not be advanced but a good rough bust might introduce a ray of skepticism into their views of regularly constituted authority, help them to stop worrying about what the country club crowd would think, and maybe provide a liberating influence.

There was a certain irony in this 75-year-old's preaching to students a quarter his age a childlike faith in America. When he should have been wearing a shawl and gaiters and doting on Ronald Reagan, he had the enthusiasm and hope and zest for the true freedom − the youth − that they were supposed to have but had somehow lost or never known.

They were not going to act on Dr. Spock's recommendation, of course. Nobody was going to dash out and get arrested for an honorable cause, risking everything.

But they listened attentively and gave his rousements a rousing hand. It wasn't every day that they were treated to such heady stuff.

9/24/78

VI
MISCELLANY

—Declined Flying Cross...

A much-decorated soldier

James Garner, the actor, and I have a thing in common, far-fetched though that might seem.

The thing is the Purple Heart, considered by many of us to be the most exalted of America's military decorations. The medal itself is heart-shaped, purple on a gold base, with a raised likeness of George Washington in heroic profile — in a word, striking, although it doesn't coordinate well with an argyle sweater.

The back of the medal says, "For Military Merit." Theoretically, you have to be wounded in combat to get one.

Garner was decorated with his Purple Heart a couple of weeks ago, the pinning being done with regular military honors. He was wounded 32 years ago while serving in Korea as a combat infantryman, known as James Bumgarner at the time. The Army often works in mysterious ways, accounting for the 32-year delay.

As Garner explained it, he was running south in Korea from enemy fire and dived head first into a foxhole. A bullet got him in the back of the lap, he said, putting it delicately.

My own military merit, attested to by the Purple Heart, was almost as glorious. I was decorated toward the end of World War II by an old friend, Buddy Douglas, a supply sergeant in the Quartermaster Corps at Fort Bragg.

A bunch of us, fresh out of prisoner-of-war camps in Germany, were being re-outfitted at Fort Bragg before going home for rest and rehabilitation.

Buddy loaded me down with khakis, olive drabs, shoes and the like. He tried to fit me with an officer's blouse but I was afraid that might be awkward, my being a Pfc. Then he said, "Okay, now what medals do you need."

I said I would take one of those Good Conduct Medals, figuring to make my mother swell with pride. I also picked a European Theater of Operations ribbon, to which I was clearly entitled, having been over there.

Buddy insisted on my taking a Unit Citation, on grounds that even if I hadn't done anything noteworthy, somebody in my outfit possibly had. The dark blue ribbon added a nice touch of color to the khakis, so I let him pin one on me.

I also accepted pilot wings, bombardier and navigator wings and a captain's bars, not to wear but as keepsakes and for post-war dating purposes.

To my everlasting credit, I drew the line at the Distinguished Flying Cross. Buddy said, "What the heck, you rode in a plane, didn't you?" I said, yes, as a radio operator-gunner, never once firing a shot in anger.

When we got around to the Purple Heart, Buddy said, "You must have got hurt over there." I said no, not really, unless you counted losing substantial weight and missing regular dental care.

Buddy said, "Didn't they bang you around, hit you in the stomach or something like that? Fellow just came through here got punched at an interrogation center and I awarded him the Purple Heart."

When the planes collided, I explained carefully, trying not to sound heroic, my machine gun tore loose from the moorings and swung around and hit me in the head.

"Knock you out?" Buddy asked. "You bleed any?"

I might have shed a drop or two, I conceded. The main thing I got was a terrible headache.

"Well, there you are," Buddy said. "Here's your Purple Heart." He pinned it on me himself and gave me a nice simulated leather case to keep it in when I wasn't on parade.

"The trouble with some of you guys," Buddy said, "is that you're too doggone modest for your own good."

The wings and captain's bars have gotten away through the years, but I am still hanging onto the Purple Heart, for the grandchildren to admire. I expect James Garner will do the same.

2/6/83

Beautify radioactive dump sites...

A modest waste proposal

The Department of Energy, in keeping with the Reagan administration policy of turning back the clock, is considering applying a venerable solution to an ultra-modern problem.

The problem is how to mark the dumps in which radioactive waste, now lying all about the country, will eventually be buried. The government doesn't want innocent citizens stumbling unaware upon the dumps, or maybe digging there for artifacts, 10,000 years from now. So, suitable markers are being considered that will withstand weathering and souvenir hunters through the ages.

A 91-page study of the world's great man-made monuments, with pictures, proposed warning symbols and the like, has been compiled to give the Department of Energy something to think about.

My grandmother and countless others of her generation had a somewhat similar problem, on a much smaller scale, of course. Their problem was what to do about full outhouse pits, to put it delicately.

Up until the 1940s, almost all of North Carolina's rural residents, of which my grandmother was one, used outhouses, also known as privies, as a convenience. The convenience consisted of a hole in the ground with a simple superstructure, most of them furnished with Sears Roebuck and Montgomery Ward catalogues, and some with crescent moons cut in the door for ventilation and decor.

After a time, the hole in the ground would fill up. Then another pit would be dug and the wooden superstructure moved to the new location. The old pit would be cooled down with a layer of lime and then covered with topsoil.

The problem in those days, as with the dumps for radioactive wastes, was how to keep the innocent from stumbling unaware into a terrible mess. They were not areas where you would want to dig for fishing worms or have the young making mud pies.

I can say from personal experience there are few things more disconcerting than to dash for the outhouse on a moonless night, in the dead of winter, wearing only longjohns and brogans, mire down ankle-deep and then sprawl headlong across a recently abandoned outhouse pit. Sympathizers, even blood relatives, tended to commiserate from a distance.

I ran into similar distress in North Africa during World War II. There were slit trenches instead of pits and no superstructures of any kind for the sake of modesty. Scurrying about during an air raid alarm, I landed spread-eagle in one of those slit trenches and wound up hors de privy, you might say.

My grandmother hit upon a simple and effective solution to the problem of what to do about old outhouse pits. To her credit, she didn't need an elaborate study, only a dip of snuff and moment's calm reflection.

She merely turned each abandoned pit into a small flower garden. The flowers practically sprang out of the ground and flourished mightily. Anybody with any sense at all would have gone through a minefield sooner than stomp through her flowers, those atop the old outhouse pits or anywhere else.

Personally I think that would be a nice touch for the radioactive waste dumps. Instead of replicas of Stonehenge or the Acropolis to mark the residue of our atomic age, leave the generations to come beds of flowers or maybe rose bushes.

If not stern warnings, they would at least be fit tokens of apology.
12/5/82

Especially against writers...

The outrageous bias of the IRS

The Internal Revenue Service, as nit-picky as ever, once again, has shown its pronounced bias against writers. The innocent victim this time is Maurice Dreicer, a food and travel writer working out of Paris, London, Rome, Hong Kong, Manila, New York, New Orleans and San Francisco. From time to time he holes up in Las Palmas in the Canary Islands to put something into writing.

For 20 years Dreicer has been gathering material for a book, to be called, *The Search for the Perfect Steak*. The search has taken him around the world three times, at enormous cost.

In a single year, for example, Dreicer's legitimate business expenses, including the upkeep of his woman secretary/traveling companion and the cost of other essential tools of the craft, came to $49,810. He claimed the business expense as an income tax deduction against his earnings, which came that year, according to my calculations, to about $75.

The Internal Revenue Service curled its lip, naturally, and disallowed the deduction. The US Tax Court, working cheek-by-jowl with the IRS, concurred in this gross miscarriage of justice.

I know how Dreicer must feel — frustrated, victimized, cheated, discriminated against — having myself been thwarted year after year by the IRS.

As it happens, I am working on a piece similar to Dreicer's book, an essay to be called, "The Search for a Steak I Can Afford." The search so far has carried me through Carrboro and along Franklin Street in Chapel Hill, at a cost of $9.60. Western Sizzlin' is ahead at the moment. Burned badly by the IRS a year ago, I plan to claim only mileage, 90 cents, for tax purposes.

Last year, when I put down 22,000 miles in unreimbursed business travel expenses, the actual count, the IRS auditor nearly fell out of her chair laughing. That is humiliating, certainly, but I will take such cackling any day over rage.

Ten years ago, after I wrote off a trip to see Carolina play in the Gator Bowl, a side-trip to Disney World and a week on the strand at New Smyrna Beach getting my notes together, I thought the IRS auditor, a different one, was going to come across the desk after me.

The officious wretch, the most uncompromising fellow I have run into, kept working his jaw muscles and gritting his teeth and clenching his fist.

Possibly the worst time I've had was in 1976, a presidential election year when I figured the IRS would be at least semi-reasonable. The auditor called everybody in the office over to look at my return and they gathered around like they were at a party or something, running their fingers down my deductions and giggling.

The IRS bias against legitimate writers is blatant. If I had put down for occupation "newspaper publisher" or maybe "TV evangelist," I expect my deductions would have sailed through without lifting anybody's eyebrow.

The publisher of a newspaper I worked for long ago used to take a world cruise every summer to recover from his rigors. He would send back home some scrawl from Capetown or Sydney or Pago Pago with orders that it be printed in the paper under his byline.

After an editor worked on the mess for a few days trying to make sense out of it, the piece would be printed. Then the publisher would write off the whole cruise as a business expense, claiming to have been exploring world opinion. As far as I know, he never heard a murmur from the IRS.

Another writer, Ernest Hemingway, killed himself in 1961, you will recall, largely out of an obsessive fear that the IRS was closing in on him. I have never entertained such a thought for even a fleeting instant, and I certainly hope Maurice Dreicer doesn't either.

7/11/82

Have a bite of 'Old Maude'...

Finding mule's place at the table

Now, with the turkey reduced to hash and Christmas menus being planned, is a good time to consider mule meat, a favorite entree of the besieged and desperately hungry.

The mule has an honored place in North Carolina, although not on the dinner table. Benson, in Johnston County, holds an annual Mule Day when this beast of intolerable burdens, including denial of parenthood and conjugal pleasures, is showered with appreciation. Ironically, the celebration takes place hard by I-95, along which traffic flies and no sensible mule would tread.

The mule's place in Southern history is fixed and secure, largely in the diary of John D. Austen, the Confederate chief telegrapher at Port Hudson, the South's last Mississippi River stronghold in the Civil War. The diary recently was presented to the state of Louisiana by Austen's descendants and is available for public consumption.

A memorable passage in the diary was entered on Port Hudson's 43rd day of siege by the Yankees. All of the meal, rice, bacon and lard were gone by then, and the gallant defenders were casting about for something to eat. That's when the lowly mule won its place in Confederate history.

"This day we had mule steak for dinner for the first time," Austen wrote. "I partook of it most heartily, and indeed found it good. It is equal at least to the poor quality of beef which we sometimes have been compelled to eat."

Port Hudson surrendered five days later, having held out for nearly a week longer than Vicksburg, probably on the strength of the mule meat.

I have to go along, up to a point, with John Austen's assessment of mule meat as table d'siege. It is indeed edible, if a trifle chewy and on the sweet side. In texture and taste it can't compare with roast cat, but is more filling. Mule sticks to your ribs, as Granny used to say of oatmeal, while cat qualifies practically as an hors d'oeuvre.

My first encounter with mule as table fare was 40 years ago when I was under siege by the Germans. Well, not exactly under siege; I was in a German prisoner-of-war camp. The fare was skimpy, depending heavily on German bread, made of sawdust and spread with denatured axle grease, and ersatz coffee, made from burned peanuts.

The arrival of the mule, on a flatbed truck, hooves sticking straight up, ready for butchering, was greeted with cheers and sustained applause, the sort of jubilation that attends the presentation of a particularly fine animal in Benson on Mule Day.

We didn't get steaks, there being about 1,000 of us having to make do with one mule. So, I can't speak with authority on that particular cut. We had a fine mule stew, garnished with a dehydrated German vegetable that turned black in water.

At times these days, dining in one of Chapel Hill's standard eating places, I look back on that mule stew with a certain longing.

The roast cat came later, at another prison camp, and was as much a lark to break the monotony as it was a game effort to ease the hunger pains.

A couple of light-hearted souls caught the stray cat, fed it for several weeks on whatever was at hand, toning up the flesh the way you top off a steer, and then held a cat roast. There wasn't enough for a genuine cat pickin'; it was more of a tasting, like at a Tupperware party. Once you get over the idea, cat isn't half-bad.

Still, everything considered, I'll take mule. There is something warm and intimate, if not altogether elegant, in saying, "I believe I'll have another helping of old Maude there."

12/2/84

Hazards of hair growers...

At least his head is clean

The Food and Drug Administration is only trying to do the right thing, no doubt, in putting the arm on preparations for growing hair.

The FDA declared that nothing on the market these days, not even the highly touted Bud pack, a mixture of topsoil and beer applied to the scalp, will prevent baldness or grow hair. So, the watchdog agency has erected a regulation to ban preparations that fail to produce the promoters' promised miracles.

The regulation on hair fertilizers becomes effective after extended public comment. I have several comments, a couple of them aggrieved.

For one thing, the timing couldn't have been worse, catching me as it did in the middle of my latest hair program.

I would have welcomed an interruption during an earlier program in 1981 that left my scalp a fiery red and my hair, the strands that survived, a sort of burnt-orange. I still have the stocking cap I was required to wear at night and look at my hair in it once in a while, sentimentally, the way parents look at their baby's hair in the scrapbook.

The latest program, orchestrated by my wife, is different in concept and in its bold promise of new hair breaking scalp within 90 days. The old lady got the idea from cable TV and conjured up visions of running her fingers through my hair and throwing away my "Bald is Beautiful" lapel button.

The cable TV pitch, a lavish production, showed men with hair practically growing on camera. Before and after pictures showed a cop with a bald spot the size of a dinner plate; new hair shrank the spot to the size of a thin dime.

Another poor wretch whose hair looked like he had been taking chemotherapy appeared in the after picture with bangs and locks covering his ears.

I got suspicious when the fellow who concocted the preparation started telling about its wonderful properties. His hair was as sparse as mine.

What cinched it for me and thrust me trembling with wild anticipation into the hair program were the accolades from newspaper columnists. Clippings from respectable newspapers were flashed one after another, telling how hair had sprung up like crab grass.

I couldn't conceive of a newspaper columnist's being conned or telling a stretcher. So I told the old lady, shoot, go ahead and order the stuff.

For the last two months I have been shampooing daily and applying cleanser and conditioner twice daily. There isn't any more hair yet and from the leavings in the shower I expect there is a net loss. But I can say with confidence that I have the cleanest head in the Piedmont and Eastern North Carolina.

There have been moments of discomfort. When I can't answer the phone or go to the door and the old lady explains that I am doing my hair, people tend to cackle. In quiet repose, when I am running through cosmic thoughts, and somebody asks what in the world I am doing, the old lady says, "Oh, he's growing hair." At such times I have to blush.

The children at home and those coming on visits inspect my scalp, fingering it gingerly, and the conversation goes: "Do you see anything?" "No, I don't see a new one?" "No, that's a piece of lint."

The deadline for the new harvest is late February. An incurable optimist, I still have high hopes. Until then, it would suit me fine if the FDA kept its confounded misgivings to itself.

1/27/85

Vignettes of a stalag...

Recalling a dismal winter

One winter we were in a stalag outside Kiefheidi, a village near the Polish border, and the weather, like the quarters, was less than charming.

In the barracks, each room housed 16 prisoners and was heated by a small coal stove. The daily ration of fuel was 16 bricks of coal, one per man.

During the day, when we could move about the compound and work up body heat, the fire was banked and kept barely alive.

In the long stretches of the night, when the cold settled in and movement about the room was severely restricted, we would rise stiffly from the floor mats from time to time and huddle in turn about the tiny stove, rubbing and beating to get the circulation going.

In the steel-gray days, when the sky seemed as low as our spirits, touch football and running, an ungainly and panting version of today's jogging, helped to ward off the cold. Partly because of that winter, I suppose, I still can't look at a jogger pumping along in Adidas and a designer sweatsuit and Walkman earphones without instant revulsion.

One of the educated among us figured out, possibly by touching his hand to his scalp, that an enormous amount of body heat was lost by not wearing a hat. And suddenly, knit caps began appearing all over the compound.

An enterprising group was turning sweaters into headgear, filling orders through an unravelling and knitting operation. Depending on the design, two or three caps could be produced from a long-sleeved sweater. A deluxe model, with bill, earflaps and chin strap, went for 20 cigarettes plus the yarn.

Among many valuable lessons in that winter of despair, I learned that lice were far better able than I was to withstand the bitter cold. Once in a while, to break the monotony and with illusions of becoming lice-free, I washed my clothes and hung them outside to freeze-dry.

Once the clothes had frozen stiff, in a couple of hours or so, not a louse could be found anywhere, in the seams or snuggled in a cuff, not even a nit. I rejoiced in the thought that I would be sleeping and walking around in my clothes without company for a while.

Then, as soon as the clothes thawed and before I could even get them on again, there those little devils would be, scampering along the inseams, whetting their appetites. They went with me all the way into France and finally said goodbye when I headed for Le Havre; they might have gone on to Paris.

One of the lighter moments in that miserable winter came with the arrival of a bomber crew still wearing khakis and Florida suntans. The crew had ditched in the Atlantic when the plane developed engine trouble.

A German sub plucked them from the briny and they were deposited in our little compound, their plans for gamboling on Miami Beach gone terribly wrong.

The winter outside Kiefheidi eventually laid me low in an unexpected way. The final blow came during one of my futile attempts at delousing.

A surprise roll-call — one of the Germans' continuing efforts to discover contraband — caught me with my clothes frozen stiff. After I stood for an hour in ankle-deep slush without socks or pants, my feet turned Carolina Blue.

Chafed and toasted by the little coal stove, the feet still refused to function properly. Not even the lice would have anything to do with them. I spent the rest of the war peeling my feet and stomping them for circulation.

Since then I have never taken winter weather seriously, especially not in North Carolina, although I still grouse about sleet from time to time, mainly to make conversation.

2/10/85

And it might help...

It won't kill you, we hope

At the time, we were huddled together, an ailing mass yearning to breathe free, in an army barracks with inside plumbing and other comforts of home, like bunks and windows.

The Russians were coming, and on one of the last nights we could hear the rumble of explosions in the distance and scatterings of small-arms fire. It didn't take a general to figure out that the situation was becoming fluid.

The main body of prisoners, about 10,000, had already been evacuated. Those of us in the barracks had been culled out because we were unable to march. We had pneumonia or frostbite or appendicitis or whatever. A few through some stroke of genius were managing simply to dog it, a risky business but worth it if you didn't get caught.

Most of the German soldiers had marched out with the main body leaving the camp deserted except for our little enclave. The German soldiers' barracks that we were in now had been converted by voice command into a field hospital. "Achtung. This barracks is now a hospital." Like that. That's how we came to be enjoying the comforts of home.

The hospital facilities were makeshift and the medical supplies scanty. There was one doctor, an American captain with frostbite so painful that he could barely hobble about.

Despite the medical shortages and his own physical discomfort, the captain's professional approach was lighthearted, some would say devil-may-care. He performed an appendectomy on a wooden table at one end of the barracks using a pocketknife for a scalpel and common thread to sew up the incision. During the operation the captain smoked a black cigar that he had scrounged somewhere, hummed and whistled and was generally jolly throughout. When he had tied the last knot with a grand flourish and cut the thread, he smiled at one of the "medics" holding the patient down and said cheerfully, "Take a look at what I cut out and see if it was an appendix."

A good many concluded that the captain wasn't exactly all there, which wouldn't have been unusual in that time and place. From then on when he asked how they felt, they would either shrink back or laugh and shout, "Fine, Doc, fine," and try to put on a healthy face.

Another time, the captain came upon a prisoner writhing on the floor. The poor fellow was clutching his stomach and between gasps pleading for help.

The captain gazed at him for a minute. In the circumstances this amounted to a careful diagnosis. He took a bottle of pills from his hip pocket, frowned in puzzlement at the label, and removed the cap and sniffed. Then he shook out a handful of pills, gave them to the fellow on the floor and said with a happy chuckle, "Take these. I don't know what they are, but if they don't kill you they might help you."

As it turned out, the pills didn't kill the poor fellow and eventually his stomach cramps went away. For all I know he's still living.

I can't say what happened to the captain when the war wound up. There was a terrible mix-up right there at the end and it was headache enough just getting back to the proper country, much less trying to keep track of what happened to everybody else.

If I had to make a guess, I would say the captain eventually got out of medicine and has become an academic or maybe a newspaper editor.
4/9/75

Memories of Manhattan...

New York: a special place

The idea of New York City going down the drain in a swirl of bad debts, defaulted bonds and broken dreams fills me with sadness and regret.

I have only warm memories of that great city, the borough of Manhattan in particular, which took me in as a callow youth, tired and poor and tempest-tossed, a huddled mass yearning to breathe free.

I was tired mainly of California, Los Angeles in particular, and had quit it in disgust at not being snapped up by the West Coast newspapers as a reporter or by the movie industry as a script writer.   '

I decided that it was only fair to give New York a chance and headed east, arriving at Times Square at 3 o'clock one morning with a typewriter, $4 and change. The Dixie Hotel took the $4 for a room for the night and the change went for breakfast at a Nedick's hot dog stand. The typewriter went into pawn for $15, stake money.

Columbia University enrolled me on the GI Bill on the spot, without wandering through the bureaucratic maze of the Veterans Administration or waiting for transcripts proving that I was higher education timber. The bursar said he would get around to those trifles in time.

Columbia's faculty club found a place for me waiting tables for meals so that I wouldn't starve, and the housing office sent me to an apartment building just off Broadway where the rent was cheap and the landlady would wait for a while.

Later the Waldorf chain of cafeterias (which had no connection and nothing in common with the hotel but the name) took me on as a night counterman, paying hard cash in addition to meals.

I spent nearly a year there, working at the Waldorf nights, occasionally going to classes at Columbia in the afternoons, and exploring New York in between times.

For a foot-loose young man with vague and shifting dreams and no clear idea of what to reach for, it was hard to conceive of a better place and time. I had the feeling, maybe unwarranted, that no matter what I might finally settle on, it was all right there, ready for the choosing, and there was no special hurry. It gave me a sense of freedom and unlimited opportunity, also perhaps unwarranted, that I had felt in no other place.

I spent most of one afternoon leaning over the railing above the skating rink at Rockefeller Plaza watching Linda Darnell, a movie star long since faded, dead now, cutting a fine figure on the ice. Another time I stood shoulder-to-shoulder with Ralph Bellamy, a celebrated stage actor in his day, in the Museum of Modern Art studying Diego Rivera's painting of the Zapatistas. Once, in a breakfast room of the Plaza Hotel where I really had no business being, I watched Walter Winchell eating a slice of melon, with his hat on. A literary agent introduced me to the men's bar at the Waldorf Astoria where I saw for the first time a waiter place an unbroken quart on the table and walk off. Those were heady moments for a young man not long out of the North Carolina Piedmont.

Those were times when you could sit in Central Park and listen to a concert, or sleep on a bench on Riverside Drive when the summer heat made a fourth-floor walkup cubicle unbearable, or doze in a subway without fear of being mugged. Those were days when a midnight stroll along Broadway or even Amsterdam Avenue was not a mortal risk but merely a matter of taking the air and gazing on the lights of the city with a certain wonder.

That was more than 25 years ago and I haven't been back since. Even so, even with the change that has wracked it, I would like to know that New York is still there.

11/2/75

Although Ike said it was okay...

POW license plate? — No thanks!

The word from the Department of Motor Vehicles that all of North Carolina's ex-prisoners of war are entitled to special license plates has got me torn in the worst kind of way.

The license plates will be red, white and blue and will be permanently assigned to those eligible and applying. Ex-POWs can switch the plates if they trade cars, a real convenience.

The reason I am torn is that the last thing in the world I want to advertise is that I am an ex-prisoner of war. I have been trying for 30 years now to live that down. I don't mind listening to war stories and I am certainly glad that the Allies won, but beyond that I try not to say much.

Riding around with a red, white and blue license plate created especially for ex-POWs would make about as much sense in my case as wearing a Stalag 3 monogram sweater or having Kriegsgefangenen tattooed on my forearms.

I have been letting the POW part of my past lie fallow since May, 1945, when General Dwight Eisenhower dropped in on some of us for a little repatriation pep talk.

About 10,000 of us were at Camp Lucky Strike, one of the centers on the Cherbourg peninsula in France where POWs were being herded together as they drifted out of Germany. Even after being de-loused, trimmed, outfitted and put on regular rations, we were still a pretty scruffy lot. Extended time in a POW camp tended to leave you a trifle worn around the edges.

Eisenhower flew in from his headquarters to welcome us back to allied control and wish us bon voyage to the states. Ike's syntax wasn't any better when he was a general in the field than after he became President, and he was in right much of a hurry that day, too, blurting his speech. I figured he was anxious to get on into Paris.

As I understood him, Ike said that it was all right for us to hold our heads up even though we had laid down our arms in the face of the enemy. The war was over anyway and nobody was going to go on blaming us for surrendering. I got the idea that the welcome back to allied control was something less than a hot embrace.

In the case of the fellow next to me, leaning on his crutches to hear Ike speak, he had laid down his arms, along with one leg and his right eye, when his B-17 exploded 24,000 feet over Berlin. Trying to buck up his spirits, I told him, "You hear that, boy? Ike says it's okay for you to hold your head up."

I have been plagued ever since with feelings of guilt about laying down my arms. When children ask me how it was in the war, I always tell them I still can't bear to talk about it. I had an uncle who used to say the same thing when I asked him about World War I. It turned out that he had been a cook in Texas and the only shooting he ever got close to was in a roadhouse near Fort Worth.

That's why I'm planning to pass up the special red, white and blue license tag, even though I'm clearly eligible. I hope the Department of Motor Vehicles will understand; I don't want to seem ungrateful.

10/15/75

A special dish...

Some facts on grits

I am not eager to get involved in the "Grits and Fritz" colloquy that was set off by somebody waving a sign at the Democratic National Convention.

Jimmy Carter says it's all right with him for the ticket to be called "Grits and Fritz" and if he doesn't object, well then, I say welcome to it. "Grits and Fritz" has a better ring to it anyway than, say, "Grin and Chin."

Somebody has got to straighten out the Associated Press, though, on what grits is (or, as the AP would put it, on what grits are). I worked for the AP for three years; measured by dog life, which in this case would be appropriate, that would amount to 21 years. So I was not surprised by the cockeyed definition of grits in the AP story out of Plains, GA.

The AP said, "Grits are a coarsely ground corn mixed with water, seasoned, cooked to a mush and served mainly at breakfast in the South." This definition is about as accurate and complete as saying that country ham is a piece of hog.

The proper making of grits is, of course, a good deal more sophisticated than simply grinding corn, mixing with water, seasoning and cooking. First, you pour the corn, hulled, into a pot or vat, depending on how many you plan to feed and for how long, and add water.

Then you add Red Devil lye. Some who are nervous about using lye often substitute wood ashes or a saline solution or both. You let this heady mixture cook until the husks separate from the kernels. With overly mature corn the cooking could take up to a couple of days.

Once the cooking is done, you wash down the corn with clean water to get rid of the lye and husks. By then the kernels will have swelled to about three times their natural size.

If you stopped right there, as some do, you would have hominy, another fine old Southern side dish that can be fried, roasted or simply heated. Personally, I prefer my hominy fried.

The transformation of hominy grits is comparatively simple. You grind the hominy and dehydrate it for packaging and storing. Then, when you feel like a mess of grits, you add water, season to taste and cook, the way the AP said.

One other thing ought to be said in connection with that AP story out of Plains. This has to do with Jimmy Carter's statement that "a lot of people equate grits with the South."

Most of the people I know, particularly those in Chatham County, equate grits with something else. When you mention "Chatham County grits," for example, they don't understand you to mean something to eat. They figure you're talking about those good ole boys who say "Saddy" for Saturday, who have gun racks and USA-1 tags on their pickups, and who would just as soon hit you in the head with a tire tool as look at you.

In the barbecue place on Highway 15-501 when the waitress says, "We get a lot of grits in here," you don't check the menu. You check the door and calculate whether you'll be able to escape in case of trouble.

Some folks I know on the coast sprinkle their conversation with references to "salt water grits." They are not talking about something you pour red-eye gravy on. They are talking about the coastal equivalent of your basic Chatham County grit. I doubt these grits were the one Carter had most people equating with the South.

There is always a lot of loose talk by candidates in presidential races, and because of the chaotic working conditions, a lot of slapdash reporting. Even so, the next time Carter and the Associated Press start messing around with grits they would do well to speak and write with more precision and care.

8/1/76

About rotten childhoods...

Treat the kids tenderly

Although I try hard not to be critical, I have to take exception to recent findings by psychologists around the country that rotten childhoods are good for you.

The way some psychologists see it, a rotten childhood is conducive to a certain invulnerability. As often as not, a child will thrive on adversity and crying need, becoming invulnerable in the process, and go on to great things.

Daniel P. Moynihan, adviser to Presidents and former United States Ambassador to the United Nations, is held up as an example. His childhood was about as pleasant and easy as 12 miles of bad road.

I happen to be an authority on rotten childhoods, having grown up in Durham during the Great Depression. Even in good times growing up in Durham has always been a trial. I figure it is some kind of penance the town is doing for the time when it was notoriously sinful, with saloons all over, a race track and a bad habit of brawling.

My own childhood was not much of a strain by Durham standards. There was always enough food, if you count leftovers. We were adequately clothed, although cautioned to walk on the grass to save shoe leather. Nobody knocked us around without cause.

In sharp contrast, the youngsters across the street had what most would say was a thoroughly rotten childhood. People in the neighborhood left food on their porch in the dead of night to keep them from starving.

Their old man gave them a terrible time, staying drunk whenever he could, and then, when he was sober, beating the boys and terrorizing the girl. After the boys began to get their growth, the beatings tapered off, mainly because they would gang up on the old man. One of them hit the old fellow in the head with a board and he was never exactly right after that, drunk or sober.

The only notable thing to come out of that rotten childhood, as far as I could tell, was the ability to fight. In fending off their old man, those boys learned how to handle themselves. The middle one, called Tarzan, after the character in a movie serial we had been following, made a name for himself all over Durham. He liked to hit people.

By the time he was 18, Tarzan was taking on full-grown millhands, several at once when he got the chance. The only one to bring him down in his prime was a fellow who pistol-whipped him from behind.

He was in his early twenties when he killed a man. He was trying to rob a produce market in Raleigh and the proprietor put up an argument. Tarzan hit him and the proprietor died. After that he was called Killer instead of Tarzan.

Somehow he got out of prison in the early part of World War II, on condition that he go into service. An officer gave him an order and Killer hit him. That landed him back in prison.

A few years ago I read in the paper that he had escaped. Those in Durham who had helped send him to prison expressed some unease. He was captured a few miles from town, armed with his fists, which long before had been ruled deadly weapons.

The last time he came up for parole, petitions were sent in from Durham, where he had grown up, and from Raleigh, where he had killed the produce man, saying please not to let him out. The parole board let him go anyway.

Killer made his last headline a couple of years ago. He was found in Raleigh in the trunk of a car, full of bullet holes.

That's why I have to take exception to the psychologists' findings. If I thought a rotten childhood was really the beginning of a wonderful future, I might start leaning heavily on our young. Instead, I think about Tarzan/Killer, and treat them as tenderly as I can.

4/25/76

Family secrets confessed...

Another sordid revelation

Joan Crawford's daughter having told the world that mommie dearest was in real life a monster, and with Bing Crosby's eldest son, Gary, now turning the dark side of old dad to public view, this seems to be a good time for me to blow the whistle on my folks.

My folks, like Joan and Bing, are long gone and incapable of any kind of rebuttal, except possibly something supernatural, maybe a haunting.

Child abuse began early for me. My folks were strolling down a street in Chattanooga, TN, in 1923, wondering idly where the next meal was coming from, when they happened upon an ice cream vendor. My sister, three at the time, wanted an ice cream cone and my old man spent his last nickel for one. I was about three months shy of birth and didn't get any ice cream at all, not even indirectly. I still haven't gotten over the blatant partiality.

The beatings began when I was an infant. In 1926 — I remember it well — Ma whacked me for throwing a bowl of oatmeal from my high chair to the floor. I can't abide oatmeal to this day.

Then, in 1929, my folks thrust me into a public school. Durham had two perfectly satisfactory private schools running that year, and Pa was pulling down $22 a week as a hotel clerk, but I got the short end again.

They did send me to a private dancing school later on, and enrolled me in the Durham Boys Choir, both of which turned out to be the severest kind of child abuse.

In 1932, Pa refused to join the World War I veterans' Bonus March on Washington. He said he had to work to put food on the table. I figured he held back just to make me look bad among the other children in the neighborhood whose fathers were camped beside the Potomac on Anacostia Flats.

Another childhood trauma came in 1936 when the Great Depression was at its grimmest. In a way it was similar to the trauma experienced by one of the Crosby sons.

According to Gary's revelations, the Crosby boys were forced to eat every morsel on their plates, on pain of being belted. One of the boys, whose appetite apparently wasn't much, hid his bacon and eggs under a rug. When the plate was discovered, Bing made the kid eat every bite, including dirt, hair and lint.

In my case, a plate of food was dropped on a rug, not hidden under it. I scraped it together for a good meal and then Ma wouldn't let me eat it.

Then there was the confrontation, psychologically scarring, over my driving privileges. I was 14 and the old man was working the night desk at the hotel. By then he was pulling down a fat $35 a week. In the afternoon, when he was taking his nap, I borrowed the car, a 1937 Dodge, to cruise up and down the alley behind our house. By any reasonable property rights, the car was as much mine as his.

On one afternoon the Dodge ricocheted off a row of garbage cans, sending a great clatter through the area. My old man came bounding out of the house in his BVDs, his eyes rolling around in his head. You would have thought the paint job cost a fortune.

The Boy Scout business wasn't nearly as bad as everybody tried to make out. The forest fire might have been out of control for a time, but it never reached the cabin, and the BB-gun shootout wasn't the least bit dangerous unless you stuck your head out.

There was no just cause for the church to disband the troop and for our fathers to carry on the way they did. It was psychically damaging to each and every one of us.

My book agent will take the calls while I am in seclusion.

3/20/83

Just call him T.F....

Names can leave a scar

The nation's psychologists have been as busy this spring as wayward Congressmen mending fences for re-election.

In just the last few weeks psychologists have presented learned papers on why it is good to have a rotten childhood, on why folks walk faster in cities than in hamlets, and on ambiverts who are unable to function effectively except under heavy pressure. A psychologist also offered a compelling argument for giving presidential candidates sanity tests. This was the most timely one in the whole bunch.

Now comes a study from a psychologist at Temple University saying that christening a child with an odd name can scar the poor thing for life. The psychologist's name is Thomas Valentine Busse, so he ought to know.

I also happen to be an authority in this area, by birth as well as through empirical research.

My father's name was Theophilus Francis Shumaker. He bore that name all his life without once seeking legal permission to change it to something like maybe Fred Smith.

This joining of Greek, English and German names was a mystery to everybody, including my grandmother who came up with Theophilus Francis. The only explanation she ever gave was that it was "different." That was true; nobody else in northern Orange County was named Theophilus Francis Shumaker.

Even though Theophilus Francis rolls trippingly off the tongue and falls soothingly on the ear, nobody ever used it. My father was called "Boots" and "Shu" and "Thee" and "T.F." He wouldn't tell anybody what his first and middle names were unless it was the government asking.

It is practically a truism to say that his name scarred him for life. He had a terrible time just learning how to spell it and I'm still not sure that he or my grandmother ever got it right. Then there was the continuing trouble through the years with trying to hide it.

I have had considerably more trouble with my surname than with the ones my parents picked out. My only memory, an indelible one, of the first grade is of little classmates shouting, "Hey, Shumaker, make me some shoes." There have also been numerous variations on the "Shu" part of the name. This scarred me.

My middle name, Hampton, hasn't caused me much trouble but it did cause some confusion. I thought I had been named after the Civil War general and I laid this claim with great pride whenever the opportunity arose. My father was a hotel man and he finally confessed that I had been named after the Wade Hampton Hotel in Columbia, SC, which he admired.

I asked why he had settled on the Wade Hampton in Columbia instead of the Zinzendorf Hotel in Winston-Salem which he also admired before it went to seed. He said that James Zinzendorf Shumaker didn't sound exactly right somehow.

Even with the deep scars my father carried and the light ones I am carrying, I figure we had it easy compared with the burdens borne by others.

There was one family in Person County that grabbed whatever was handy at the moment as names for the children. One of the boys was named U.S. Mail Jones.

The family enjoyed getting mail and everybody was fond of the green truck with gold lettering that frequently stopped out front. If U.S. Mail is alive today and aware of the postal service he ought to be blushing with shame.

Another one was named Slick When Wet Jones, after a highway sign. He probably was called Slick, which isn't too bad when you stop and think about it.

The one I liked best was one of the girls' names, Dangerous Curve Ahead Jones. She was bound to have been scarred, but aside from that I have often wondered how she turned out.

5/30/76

Despite stark setting...
POWs had Christmas spirit

Nobody asked me, unless you count the radio announcer who called bright and early and said in dulcet tones, "Would you like to recall for our listening audience, sir, the most memorable Christmas you ever had?"

Having a somewhat strangled public-speaking voice and not being given to talking on the telephone any more than is necessary, I declined to recall.

Later on I felt a twinge of guilt. After all, this is the season of giving, and what could be more generous and warm-spirited than sharing one of my Christmases past. What indeed?

Memorable is not the right word for it. Vivid would be better, or maybe stark.

It was 30 years ago, in 1944. There were about 10,000 of us, a motley collection of Americans, Canadians, English, South Africans, Scots, Sons of Eire, with a few Russians thrown in for an Asiatic touch.

The camp was near the village of Kiefheidi, 90 miles northeast of Berlin. It consisted of roughly 10 acres enclosed by fences and barbed wire, with guard towers at regular intervals.

During the summer several hundred of us had lived in tents while more barracks were being built. When the Baltic winter began settling in, we moved inside and that was a comfort of sorts.

The holiday season was formally opened with a visit by Max Schmeling, the former world heavyweight champion. He had become a gentleman farmer after retirement from the ring and was the most affable German, the only affable German, we had run into.

A bold spirit among us shouted, "Wait'll Joe Louis gets hold of you again," and Schmeling covered his head with his arms and then joined in the laughter. Nobody could figure out what Max Schmeling was doing touring POW camps. The way the war was going, it would have made more sense for him to be spreading Christmas cheer among German troops. Though puzzled, we accepted his visit with good grace and wished him a Merry Christmas.

Christmas itself that year was what others would call scrimpy and forlorn. It was fat and joyful by our everyday standards.

A Christmas gift shop did a brisk business in one of the barracks. Some ingenious souls had unraveled sweaters and used the yarn to knit a striking array of caps. There were hand-carvings, paintings, hand-tooled leather goods, and unaccountably, an assortment of jellies and jams. The gift shop proprietors refused to say how the jellies and jams got in there. Free enterprise manages to survive all kinds of adversity. The medium of exchange was that universal wartime currency, cigarettes.

A few days before Christmas we were sent through the Germans' private wash house and luxuriated for once in showers and then were given a change of clothes. Later on we learned that this was for the good of the Fatherland, not a Christmas present to us. They wanted our uniforms to use in the Battle of the Bulge, not knowing that then, it was nice just to be shed of the lice for a while.

Early Christmas morning two trucks came into our compound and headed for the cook shack. We counted 16 legs sticking up and a great cheer arose. We figured to be eating high on the horse that day — four horses. And we did.

The Germans threw in a few extra loaves of ersatz bread, a strange concoction with the texture of sawdust; extra ersatz coffee, a brew that tasted like burned peanuts; and extra measures of an exotic seaweed soup. I nearly foundered myself.

That afternoon the Germans released some of our mail, not the packages, of course, just letters. Those who didn't get any, which was most of us, read other people's with great interest.

Before they locked us up and brought in the dogs for the night, the C Compound Christmas Carolers went from barracks to barracks singing those fine old Yuletide standards. The carolers weren't Fred Waring's Pennsylvanians, but they had practiced hard and were pretty good.

When they went into "Silent Night" a lot of grown men swallowed hard and looked away or studied the ceiling. After the carolers finished there was nose-blowing all over the place.

The spirit of Christmas might have seemed incongruous in that place where life was cheap, surrender to animal instincts easy, and the constant concern mere survival. But it came, and in a way it was amazing.

Personally, given a choice, I prefer the kind we have now.
12/18/74

It had a settling effect...

'Onward Christian Soldiers'

At various times in between my Baptistism, Presbyterianism, Episcopalianism and a brief shot at Catholicism, in a sort of one-soul ecumenical movement, I have been partial to the Methodist Church.

The first suit I ever owned, at age 5, a double-breasted tweed with knickers — tie and breast-pocket show handkerchief thrown in free for good will — got its trial run and longest use at the old Lakewood Methodist Church in Durham, Sunday school and regular service.

It was at Lakewood, in a congregation made up largely of Liggett & Myers tobacco workers, a few bootleggers and other free enterprisers, department store clerks and the proud unemployed, that I got taken with sprinkling. At practically every altar call, unless physically restrained, I marched up there with the newly converted, knickers hiking above my knees as I began to get my growth, and knelt on the velvet for a refreshing dampening.

I finally cut back on the altar calls when my mother, after trying everything else, said if I didn't knock it off the sprinkling would shrink my new suit. In those days suits remained new until outgrown.

Later, in my Baptist years, sprinkling seemed on reflection to be an overly casual embrace of the faith. A few drops on the head, or for that matter anything less than a hurricane seemed a trifle tame after a triple-dipping in the Mighty Eno River.

It was also at Lakewood Methodist that I developed my Sunday school manners — later polished at Watts Street Baptist where the teacher broke into tears weekly — and my hymn-singing voice, a strangled soprano at the time.

Sunday school for my age group consisted mainly of running around the parsonage, where the class was held, hollering and screaming and dodging adults who kept trying to hit us. About the only way to get us into semi-formal array was for the teacher to sit down at the old upright piano and begin banging away.

There was little to choose between the hollering and singing but, to the teacher's credit, we stayed in place. That was my introduction to "Onward Christian Soldiers."

Now there was a hymn, unlike "Sweet Hour of Prayer" and some of the others, where you could really blast away, get your whole self into it, so to speak, and work off a lot of youthful zest and energy. The Sunday school teacher turned to it regularly as the hymn of last resort.

To say that we were transported by "Onward Christian Soldiers" would be to overstate the case, slightly. But it did have a calming effect in Sunday school, leaving us wrung out, and on those auspicious occasions when it was called during regular church services it helped to bring the young out of their stupors.

About the only time I got smiled upon beatifically in church, instead of being pinched hard or thumped on the head, was when I was putting everything I had into "Onward Christian Soldiers."

In my adult years at Amity Methodist in Chapel Hill, I went at "Onward Christian Soldiers" with the same gusto, causing some in the congregation to turn around and look and my family to edge away, pretending they weren't with me.

To this day, given a choice of everything in the hymnal, I would take "Onward Christian Soldiers," after "Amazing Grace" and "Just As I Am" and "Bringing In The Sheaves" and a few others. That solid beat, the up-and-down on "soldiers," and all-around musicality put it far and away ahead of, say "Jesus Loves Me," to my mind.

So, you can imagine my dismay and that of countless others to learn that a committee of the United Methodist Church hymnal revisionists, plans to pull "Onward Christ Soldiers" out of the repertoire. The complaint is that

the hymn smacks of militarism almost as much as "The Halls of Monte-
zuma" and "The Caissons Go Rolling Along."

I figure I turned Baptist just in time.

6/8/86

And that's not all bad, either...
Today's kids have it easy

One of those truisms that trip casually off the tongues of graybeards and
fall only lightly on the ears of the young, if at all, lit the dusk the other day.

It came from Gov. Richard Lamm of Colorado, who sees young Americans as having grown soft in their lives of wealth and luxury: "You know,
the hungry lion hunts best. Our kids have ceased to be hungry."

I don't know about hungry lions and will take the governor's word about
them. But I can speak with authority for kids, having been one.

As I see it, the idea of deprivation building character is about as sound as
the idea of varsity football at the University of Oklahoma toning up the
moral fiber. Hard work, from what I have seen and known, is not nearly as
ennobling as many self-made souls like to say. And going hungry, while
possibly sharpening the sense of smell and developing an urge to steal, is
mostly painful.

Children of the Great Depression, of which I was one, are especially
lavish in their praise of the hard work ethic and of making do at roughly the
survival level. They never let their own young forget, while packing them
off to Duke or Davidson or the University in Chapel Hill, that they had to
walk five miles through snow and ice to a one-room schoolhouse.

A father from the Great Depression, buying his son a pair of shoes is apt
to say, "When I was your age my folks made me walk on the grass to save
the soles." Or, "If I needed a new pair of shoes I had to scrounge empty
bottles for refunds until I had the money."

A child of today, sniffing at the turnip greens and razzing the carrots, is
told that in the old days you didn't leave the table until your plate was clean,
if you had to sit there all night. Leftovers were returned to the table again
and again, until they were eaten or began to germinate.

Nowadays, Junior asks for a new car and, while checking the dealerships, old dad says if he had so much as asked for use of the family car his old man would have decked him or had him committed.

Today's parents, helping their young sort out their credit cards, recall that when, as children themselves, they asked for maybe a Moon Pie and a Pepsi, they were told to get a job. At age 9? Of course. Mow lawns.

Those who went through those hard and mean years half a century ago still have vivid memories, and the memories affect them in many ways. Some vow to see that their children will have it far better, and so they lay on the luxuries and make possible the soft and easy life of which Gov. Lamm complained.

Others of us, permanently scarred by hard times when young, still can't spend discretionary money without emotional turmoil. We can't leave a morsel on a plate without suffering guilt, and regardless of all other considerations, have only contempt for the idle rich. Any money that comes easily arouses deep suspicion.

And, of course, we recite the generational wisdom about how today's young have grown soft and lazy and the country is going to hell in a handbasket.

Looking back down the years at my generation in the Depression and then at today's young, of whom I see dozens every weekday, and making something other than an invidious comparison, I would take the new crop.

That's one of many reasons why I will never be elected governor.

9/7/86

To write novel, run weekly paper...

A newsman's two dreams

Every newspaperman who sticks to his last, deaf to the siren songs of public relations and politics and television and corporate communications, eventually comes to nurse one of two dreams; in extreme cases, both of them.

One of the dreams is to write a best-selling novel. There are by accurate count enough unfinished novels in newsrooms across the country to keep a bonfire the size of Mt. Kilimanjaro going for several years, which might be a good idea.

The other dream is to run a weekly newspaper in a small community on the order, in all-around probity and friendliness, of Andy Griffith's Mayberry. The dream envisions the editor as conscience of the community, resident philosopher, watchdog of government and commerce.

I speak with unassailable authority here, having nursed both of the dreams at one time or another through the years, sometimes both of them at once.

I have several unfinished novels scattered about, not counting one that was eaten by rats in a barn in Chatham County. I also have been working for more than 30 years on a massive semi-autobiographical novel similar to *Look Homeward, Angel*. Nothing on paper, of course, but numerous truly gripping scenes sketched out in my mind.

The late Charles Craven, who nursed the best-seller dream for many years, said the happiest moment of his newspaper career was when he finally decided that he didn't really have to write a novel. I take a certain solace from his concession and now go at my novel-writing casually.

I actually realized the weekly newspaper dream, a few flashes of which turned out to be heavenly and many nightmarish. I can recall but one heavenly moment without consulting my notes, which seem to have been misplaced. The one moment of exhilaration I remember vividly was when a reader whose judgment I respected said that he admired sincerely our decision not to run court dockets, especially the one in which his name appeared for drunk driving.

It is much easier to recollect the name-calling, threats of bodily harm, advertiser boycotts and social opprobrium that went naturally, I figured at the time, with weekly newspapering.

The thing that disconcerted me most was the boulder, weighing close to a ton, that I found in my office one morning. The boulder was left as a comment on how one of the paper's editorials had flown. I never could figure out how in the world the critic was able to get the thing in there. It took four burly fellows and two dollies to haul it off.

Weekly newspapers, I discovered from experience and scholarly research, divide roughly into three categories.

There are those whose main role is that of community booster, accentuating the positive, ignoring or at most handling gingerly the negative, extolling public and private virtue. They are usually financially successful and long-lived.

Then there are the troublemakers, forever raising Cain about one outrage or another, finding public and private fault, agitating for change and generally fretting the readership. Their spans are often vagrant – here today, gone tomorrow, and with little visible means of support.

And then there are those notable exceptions that combine a nicely controlled crusading zeal with community respectability. They alternately flourish and fall on lean times, depending on how nicely the crusading zeal is controlled.

Ken Fortenberry, lately of the *McCormick* (SC) *Messenger*, clearly fell into the hell-raising category. His story of being squeezed financially and terrorized personally has been told by daily newspapers throughout the territory, in the *New York Times*, and on the front page of the *Philadelphia Inquirer*.

Now he is in Columbia, in public relations, the final workplace, for many former innocents come of age, where, in comparative serenity, he can sort out his busted dream and maybe work on the other one, writing a novel.

2/22/87

Virtues of muckraking...

An issue of newspaper ethics

The first time I ran into a serious problem of newspaper ethics was at the *Durham Morning Herald* in the long-gone days when muckraking was counted a shining virtue.

A reporter assigned to do a story on Durham's sinful ways visited all the bootleggers he could find, buying a pint at each sinkpit. When his story appeared – not exactly an expose, since everybody knew about the bootleggers anyway – the bootleggers cried foul. They said it wasn't fair for a reporter to come in that way, posing as a regular toper.

The assignment raised another ethical question, somewhat less serious. Should the reporter be allowed to drink the whiskey he had gathered? The publisher demurred and the whiskey disappeared. I was told it was donated to a hospital for medicinal use, maybe for snakebites.

The *Herald* also had to contend with ethical problems created by Hank Messick, a reporter who went on to become a nationally celebrated muckraker.

Hank began his muckraking career in Durham by exploring a city official's garage to see if the fellow had confused any of the city's belongings with his own. That method of reporting stirred such official wrath that Hank had to be transferred from Durham's City Hall beat to the paper's bureau in Chapel Hill.

This was a peaceful village then, compared with nowadays, and Hank attracted attention right off. He discovered by some kind of extrapolation and triangulation a sex-and-drinking club in the basement of University Baptist Church involving offspring of most of the notables in town. That story never came close to seeing print, being scorching-hot to the touch, but Hank's investigative reporting – going around town asking questions that made people blush – caused a couple of *Herald* editors to blanch and take a drink.

Hank once jumped out of hiding to photograph Orange County's member of the state House of Representatives, one of Chapel Hill's most beloved public figures, coming out of the ABC store in Morrisville with an armload of liquor. The photo and accompanying story were quickly killed in keeping with good newspaper ethics.

At the peak of his career, Hank posed in Miami as an underworld figure from Detroit interested in setting up a string of whorehouses in Dade County. His stories resulting from that deception appeared in the *Miami Herald*, the same newspaper that did the enterprise reporting on Gary Hart.

Not to boast about it or apologize for it, but I have been involved, directly or indirectly, in trespassing, breaking and entering, misrepresentation, white-lying and going through people's trash cans in search of news. My own transgressions were for a greater good, I figured then, with the ends justifying the means. I still feel that way about some of them, especially the one involving trespassing and breaking and entering.

The Ku Klux Klan was exerting considerable influence in Hillsborough at the time, conducting a "trade with a Klansman" drive among merchants and flashing KKK bumper stickers. A reporter and photographer I was responsible for broke into the Klan headquarters and photographed the membership roll and copied the minutes of the meetings.

Our newspaper, a game little weekly, put the membership roll on the front page and those Klansmen disappeared into the slash pine. Nobody was interested in filing trespass and breaking and entering charges against us.

5/10/87

The glob and the bag...

Sure cures for hiccups

Out of simple human kindness and consideration, I am not going to tell anybody except blood-kin about my operation.

In my long experience I have found that one of the quickest ways to clear a room is to say, "Let me tell you about my operation." Those who don't leave at a half-trot or can't lurch up out of their chairs, their eyes glaze over and their heads droop.

I'm not going to show my scars, either, to anybody outside the immediate family. I still remember Lyndon Johnson, when he was President, hiking up his shirt to show off his surgical scar. It gave several people I know the dry heaves.

But I would like to mention the hiccups.

Every time I undergo deep surgery (twice) I come out of the anesthesia with an extended case of hiccups.

The first time was about 12 years ago, following an appendectomy. The appendix had burst and peritonitis set in. After the surgery I had tubes running through my nose, down my gullet and into the stomach. I also had hiccups.

Finally the tubes came out. The hiccups continued for 10 days, exciting all kinds of sympathy and home remedies and sure-cures.

The best-known cure, scaring the daylights out of the hiccupper, wasn't allowed, on grounds that it went against acceptable medical procedures.

Hollering suddenly, popping paper bags and the like also tended to upset other patients on the floor.

I went along with most of the other suggestions: breathing into and out of a paper bag; holding my breath until I turned blue and then gulping nine swallows of water; putting my head in a grocery bag and holding it tight around my neck until particles began to swim before my eyes; and holding my nose and popping my ears the way travelers are supposed to do on planes.

A couple of suggested cures were more than I could manage. One was bending way over and drinking water from the back side of the glass. The water kept running out my nose and nearly drowned me.

The other abject failure was self-hypnosis. Every time I would get about halfway into a trance somebody would come in and say, "How are the hiccups, you poor thing," and there they would go again.

The hiccups finally just went away after that surgery 12 years ago, mainly, I figured, because I had to get back to work.

This time the hiccups lasted for just under two weeks, setting a new personal record and bringing forth two cures I had never heard of. One cure was to get liquored-up on caraway brandy — not sloppy or roaring or knee-walking drunk, just pleasantly smashed.

I had never touched caraway brandy to know what I was drinking and the clerk at the ABC told my daughter his store had never stocked it but he could probably special-order it since this was a medical emergency. My daughter figured that would take too long to do my hiccups any good.

The other recommended cure was called the Peanut Butter Glob. It came from a nurse wise beyond her years and with broad experience in hiccups.

You take a glob of peanut butter about the size of a ping-pong ball and put it on the back of your tongue. Then you work it around, taking care not to strangle yourself, until you have eaten the whole glob.

It worked the first time; the hiccups disappeared, never to return. In the meantime I have lighted several candles for the nurse and mention her favorably at every appropriate chance.

I am also putting together a multi-million dollar proposal to be presented to the Upjohn Co. or Johnson and Johnson or Burroughs Wellcome, places like that.

4/26/87

On returning to The Hill...

The twice-a-year shock

The culture shock, the shock of recognition, whatever it is, comes twice a year — in the fall, after the long, hot summer, and in January, after the month-long Christmas break.

For one coming back to Chapel Hill after an extended stay on Caswell Beach, a spit of sand three miles long and two rows of houses wide, the difference is astonishing, roughly the difference between Saturday night and Sunday morning.

First, there is the difference in terrain, from the flatlands of the Coastal

Plains to the hills and valleys of the Piedmont. On Caswell and its environs, the only promontories are the dunes and the spoil areas along the Intracoastal, the dredgings left by the Corps of Engineers.

After weeks on that sandy spit, the hills of Orange, among which we once lived, and Edwards Mountain in Chatham County, along whose ridges we once had a place, seem to tower like Everest, or anyway Anapurna.

Then there is the sky. On the island, the big sheltering sky seems as limitless as the Atlantic, and those who stay there for more than two weeks in summer check it constantly — for overcast and sunshine and rain and signs of dangerous weather, at night for the moon and the stars, and in late summer and fall and early winter for those violent sunsets with the sun a ball of fire slipping into the sea.

In Chapel Hill, when you notice the sky at all it is through oak limbs and leaves and between high rises and condos, and then, for the academic mind, it is mainly to see if it is falling. An uncluttered view of the sunset can be had, I am told, from the top of the Bell Tower and, for those able to shinny up it, from the University's television transmission tower.

Coming onto Oak Island from the mainland, across the Intracoastal, if you look slightly to the left and right, you get the same view that greeted the first settlers — broad sweeps of marsh and tidal creeks, live oak and yaupon, and the Cape Fear in the mists in the middle-distance.

Coming into Chapel Hill, nothing seems the same. Last summer's open field is a shopping mall or townhouses or an office complex, and a creek along the old hiking trail is now beneath a stretch of interstate highway. Yesterday's combo filling station/barbecue joint has disappeared in favor of a hotel that looks as if it had been transported in one piece from the French Riviera.

On Caswell in mid-January the unwritten rule of the road seems to be one car at a time. At the sound of a car in the distance, you go to the window, if you have any curiosity at all, to see what in the world is going on, or maybe step out on the deck to wave, sometimes at strangers; it doesn't matter.

In Chapel Hill, there seems to be an ordinance or possible unanimous agreement among townspeople and students that every car in town must be lane-hopping down the streets or in public parking places at all times of day and night, 365 days a year, preferably with horns blowing and motors revving. If anyone stepped out on a porch to wave at a stranger the authorities would probably try to have the poor soul committed.

Caswell residents stroll along the strand, passing the time of day, if they are in a garrulous mood, with anybody who happens by, much in the way that small-town residents strolled Main Street in the days when strolling was socially acceptable and casual conversation wasn't a terrible strain.

On Chapel Hill's downtown Franklin Street, which used to compare favorably in the social graces with Caswell's strand, people will walk up your back if you're not careful and you can get swept along to places you never intended to go. The standard sidewalk conversation is a holler into a cupped ear.

If it weren't for my amazing adaptability in shifting from one place to the other, I would probably be confused.

1/17/88

'improvements' ruined it...

Farewell to The Shack

The Shack, on downtown Rosemary Street, last week was reduced to an empty shell, front door and window stripped away, roof more swaybacked than ever, waiting only to be razed or cave in, whichever came first.

Inside there remained only the debris of 35 years or so of casual drinking and socializing: empty beer cans and bottles and caps, an overturned table, part of a ripped-out booth, a smashed Budweiser clock, a soggy paperback book on the concrete slab floor. A mongrel sniffed among the ruins.

The last proprietor of The Shack, someone called "Wheaties," had already quit the premises and town. No one seemed to know why The Shack was finally giving up its ghost. There was unanimous agreement that, unlike those times in the past when The Shack had appeared to be terminal, the end was now at hand. The general surmise was that the successor would be another parking lot.

For many, the ignoble end last week was merely a belated coup de gras. As the purists saw it, The Shack died 15 years ago with the arrival of a television set, pinball machine, telephone, dart board, jukebox and fraternity and sorority carousers.

Personally, I mark the beginning of the decline and fall of The Shack from a night in 1962 when an impatient wife entered the place and urged her husband to come home by spraying him with Mace. This breach of etiquette had a profound effect on numerous husbands present, in addition to the victim; the ambience of The Shack never was the same thereafter.

Up until then The Shack had been an oasis in the hurly-burly of Chapel Hill, a sanctuary in the midst of the madding crowd and yet well insulated against it. The place was restful, periodically calm, conducive to conversation, deep thought and serious beer drinking.

Brack Creel, the original and most celebrated proprietor, a milk drinker himself on account of ulcers, provided a free circulating library for those who would rather read than talk. Benches and chairs were arrayed in one corner behind the coal stove and along the wall behind the counter and drink boxes for those mainly interested in government and conversant with politics.

The booths were for small seminars, informal university classes, alumni meetings, business appointments, off-color debates, afternoon naps and the like. A radio, the only concession besides electricity to 20th century amenities, was used exclusively for sports broadcasts and election returns.

There were certain rules, largely understood and firmly enforced. One obscenity could not be used as a verb, another one as a noun. (Brack had a feel for the language.) The presence of women was to be tolerated but not encouraged. Regulars were not to be disturbed during naps unless their wives were outside in the parking lot blowing the horn.

Such as it was, a center of civility and amiability, a place where strong character could assert itself, The Shack attracted a wildly mixed clientele — the famous and the obscure, intellectuals and those blessed mostly with native cunning, the pious and the profane, the lecturers and those who sat quietly listening and sipping. A retired Metropolitan Opera star, a professor, a precinct captain, a truck driver and a professional bum — the cream and the dregs of Chapel Hill society — could always find common ground in The Shack.

After Brack Creel died, his brother-in-law and then the brother-in-law's son kept the Shack going for a while in the old tradition. The regulars were being thinned out, by death and other transfiguration, but the plastic and neon were still in the distance.

Then an enterprising young promoter got hold of The Shack and began making "improvements" to broaden the appeal and deepen the take.

Maybe they will name the successor the Brack Creel Memorial Parking Lot.

5/20/79

A requiem of reunion regrets...

We aren't the way we were

The announcement of the 40th reunion warned that the country club where the festivities would be held required gents to wear coats and ties. That will give you an idea of the class, as well as the tone and dignity of the Durham High School Class of '41.

The country club was a sleek complex of tennis courts, golf course, Olympic swimming pool, parking lots and neo-Colonial clubhouse with veranda. It was surrounded by neo-Georgian and neo-colonial homes in the $200,000 range. On my last inspection of the area, as a callow youth, the place had been slash-pine and broomstraw country.

Hostesses pinned name tags on us in the foyer and each one had a picture reproduced from the high school annual showing how the wearer looked 40 years ago. Mine showed a thick head of hair, clear eyes, cherubic face and eager grin — the way I still see myself sometimes when the bathroom mirror is fogged.

The popular practice at the reunion was to cover your nametag with your hand and say to someone out of the long ago, "Guess who I am?" After four straight misses I guessed that everybody was Pudlucas, a tramp who once lived in a shack by the railroad tracks in downtown Durham and did impromptu shuffle-dances for small change.

I almost left the premises after three old classmates, one after another, peered at my name tag and said they thought I was dead. One looked me over and said gently, "You've been sick, haven't you?"

A matronly lady with Carolina blue hair, lightly corseted, heavily powdered and rouged, laid a hand like a garden tool on my arm and shrieked, "Jimmy Shumaker," startling those within shouting distance. "You're not Jimmy Shumaker," she yelled. "Ah, c'mon, you're not Jimmy Shumaker." Caught cold and slightly stunned, I swore that I was, all the while trying to figure out who in the world she might be. After sneaking a glance at her name tag, I remembered a willowy blonde I had spent most of my waking hours with 40 years ago, vowing eternal love. In those days she was Southern belle to the marrow, giving "war" three syllables (as in "I don't want you goin' off to any old wah-uh-wah"). Now, after 35 years in New Jersey, she was city-wise and her hoarse chatter fell on the ear like a stream of gravel.

Possibly out of some tribal instinct or a sudden remembrance of shared values, the old cliques of high school days reformed in tight circles, on the veranda, in far corners and at the bar. I wandered around, as I did at high school social gatherings, semi-lost.

During the banquet a class officer called the roll of achievers – doctors, lawyers, a three-star admiral, presidents and executive vice presidents of corporations. One of the doctors, a celebrated surgeon, sat in imperial solitude, ready to receive. My wife said, "Why haven't you ever done anything?"

Then the speaker, trying to give a light touch to the proceedings, read from a column I had written for the high school newspaper. I slid down deep in my chair and covered my face with a napkin.

After the banquet, members of the championship basketball team gathered to replay moments of triumph, one demonstrating, for those who might have forgotten, his fallaway jumpshot. Members of the championship football team were more restrained, most of them having taken on a substantial girth.

The band, led by a Durham High graduate now gainfully employed as a piano player in California, swung into "In the Mood" and there was a great gyration of bodies flinging sore-footed about the dance floor. One old party staggered back to the table, ashen-faced and breathing hard, and said, "That could give a fellow a heart attack."

Members of the Class of '41 voted overwhelmingly to reunite again in five years when those still around would be in their 60s. I abstained.

1/28/81

ERA didn't have a chance...
They came with Bibles

Back in the mid-1960s Terry Sanford toyed briefly with the idea of wresting a US Senate seat from Sam Ervin, which, looking back, doesn't seem to have been the most sensible thing in the world to try to do.

Sanford consulted several muses, held a damp finger to the wind – a northeaster was blowing at the time – and decided that the idea wasn't so hot after all. "How in the world can you beat a man," he concluded, "who's holding the Constitution in one hand and the Bible in the other?"

How, indeed?

Twenty-four members of the NC Senate and others across the state lathering for the equal rights amendment might well be asking themselves now, with equal wonder, how in the world can you beat a woman who's holding the Bible in one hand, a mess of fried chicken wrapped in foil in the other, and is wearing a double-knit pantsuit and a beehive hairdo.

Obviously, you don't. No prudent soul would try.

I didn't arrive at the Legislative Building until around 10 last Tuesday morning and by then there were only a few from the anti-ERA forces still deployed outside, passing out tracts. The first tract was pressed on me by a lady with glittering eyes and clenched teeth. She was wearing a bright red anti-ERA placard in the shape of a stop sign about a foot wide. The tract was entitled "Friend" and the first chapter began, "You need to be saved...." I couldn't argue with that.

The scene in the rotunda was a dead-ringer for the homecoming at Mt. Hermon Baptist many years ago, the time it rained. Folks milled around, Bibles tucked under their arms to give their hands free play, munching fried chicken and talking as hard as they could. A lady from near Wilson offered me some lunch and I selected a drumstick.

The anti-ERA forces had seized the high ground, the Senate galleries, around 8 that morning and by noon, with the Senate session still an hour away, were getting restless. I stood in one of the gallery doorways to count the house and almost became a casualty. A lady wearing a hat made of Stop ERA signs flung me aside with a flick of her hips. I am a sleek 180 and she had me by about 60 pounds. I came down on the side of ERA then and there. If this country ever has another war, I would feel a whole lot better knowing that she was out there fighting.

About 15 minutes before the Senate convened a fellow took the floor of the chamber and warned those in the galleries about demonstrating. He said he didn't want to see anybody ripping out the guard rails and that amens and hallelujahs would have to be muted, or words to that effect.

After the Senate convened, Lt. Gov. Jimmy Green, who presides in there, said pretty much the same thing. He said if they didn't behave he would kick everybody out. You could hear teeth clicking all around.

The high point of the historic ERA debate came, so far as I could tell, when Sen. Bobby Lee Combs solved a vexatious problem. He had received telephone calls from President and Rosalynn Carter and chatted with the

Governor about ERA. The problem was how to work that into the debate while the TV cameras were grinding and the newspaper wretches were taking notes.

Sen. Combs solved the problem by rising on a point of personal privilege, denouncing anybody who figured he was being pressured by President Carter, Rosalynn and the Governor. They were all good, close, personal friends, he said, and had called mainly to see how he was getting along. Anybody who said he was being pressured was a confounded liar, or words to that effect.

The debate was all downhill after that, except for two other stirring moments. One came when Sen. Craig Lawing of Mecklenburg said he had faith in our form of government. That made the hairs stand up on the back of my neck and sent tingles up and down my spine.

The other shimmering moment came during a speech by an Honorable I couldn't see because an anti-ERA woman with hulking shoulders hove-to in front of me. This astral voice said that even though ERA was angelic the whole thing didn't amount to doodleysquat and life would go on pretty much as before in the NC State Senate.

I am willing to believe that.

3/6/77

Motors play fortissimo...

UNC has a concert by cars

With the heavy de-emphasis of football in Chapel Hill, UNC students have been diverting themselves this fall in new ways, some of them creative.

Several have been down here chasing rabbits, although that is not new or particularly creative. There have also been more students than usual at the Sertoma Club's weekly turkey shoot.

Some students, making up for the football season, have gone into transcendental meditation. I have heard that a few also have turned to studies, but I am not inclined to put much stock in that.

The most creative divertissement anybody has spotted so far was a concert given in a parking lot on the UNC campus. This was the Southeastern premiere of a new work, and it came right after a speech by UNC President William Friday telling how good higher learning was doing under reorganization.

Anybody could go to the concert free; in fact, all you had to do was walk through the parking lot. I went because I heard a terrible commotion and ran over there to see if anybody was hurt.

The name of the concert is "Car Bibbe," and it was composed by a Swede named Al Hansen. As best I can make out from the program notes, Hansen claims to have been inspired by Richard Petty.

Four performers were listed in the program on instruments including a 1969 Volvo, a 1966 Rambler, a 1971 Pinto and a 1970 Ambassador. Special thanks was paid to W.S. Newman, Alumni Distinguished Professor of Music, who was in charge of tuning.

By the time I arrived on the scene there must have been a couple of hundred students in the audience, all smiling. The conductor was David Boelzner, a graduate student in music. He was wearing a tuxedo and motorcycle helmet and was standing on a stone wall. The performers were parked in a line in front of him, with their scores clipped to the sun visors.

The conductor spread his score on a music stand, flung his locks into place on his shoulders, rapped his baton, lifted his arms, and the commotion broke loose again.

One performer, when it was his turn to come in, started up his car, racing the motor according to the score. Another performer jumped out and banged his hood and trunk lid up and down. Another performer, a percussionist, slammed her car doors time and again. Another one, who I figured was in the wind section, sat in her car triple-fingering the horn. Boelzner stood up there conducting the whole thing, drawing out the horn, hushing the car doors, urging the racing motor into a haunting refrain.

The concert took a little getting used to at first, particularly if you were trying to follow the music without a score. After a while, though, you could appreciate what the composer was getting at — a glorious attempt to transcend the limitations and insensitivity of man's inhumanity to machine, as Hansen put it — and see that it wasn't just another Chapel Hill traffic jam.

A performer, Andre Barbera, claimed after the concert that all of them were accomplished musicians. Maestro Boelzner had once parked cars at a pizzeria in Two Eggs, FL.

Craig Lister had once played Beethoven's *Fifth Symphony* with a

Toronado and Mustang, and Gloria Fernandez received her early training in driver education school. Barbera himself won fame and critical acclaim for a 1971 performance of Ligeti's *Second String Quartet*, which resulted in $750 in damages to a Buick, a Pontiac and a VW squareback.

I asked one of the performers as he was getting ready to drive his instrument away if any thought had been given to holding a concert during halftime at one of Carolina's football games, to liven the stadium up a little. He said no, his group didn't believe in mixing fine art with amateur sports.
11/19/75

Yule-tidings from us...
Those family greetings...

To relieve the post-Christmas fantods, also known as the yuletide blacks, I generally get out season's greetings I have been collecting over the years and read them through, glowing inwardly all the while.

My collection is highly selective, with none of your Currier & Ives or Grandma Moses cards. There is not a New England snow scene with a steepled country church in the lot. My collection is made up entirely of Christmas "letters" in which families caught us up on what everybody had been doing the past year.

Most are mimeographed, some with red ink on green paper, some with green ink on red paper. There are a couple in black ink on white paper which I figured were run off in state offices in the interest of economy.

The average length is about one legal-size page, single-spaced. There is one here that runs two and a half pages, but is not what you would call windy. It came from a large and hyper-active family and the space was needed to tell fully what every member had been up to.

I have worked up a composite greeting fairly representative of the whole lot, and it begins like this: "Wonderful friends near and far – All during the year we think of you fondly and welcome your letters, calls and visits, and at this season your Christmas gifts and news. The news from the Smiths in 1975 didn't make bold headlines, but we know you'll be interested all the same ..."

They go on to report in charming detail what each member of the family did during the preceding year. "Our Clyde" completed his internship in the White House and has returned to law school at Harvard. "Our Suzy" made her debut and is trying to decide between Smith and Vassar. Father Ed was promoted to executive vice president and Mother Eleanor was elected precinct vice chairman.

Every Christmas letter in my collection is from a wonderful, All-American family whose achievements are downright inspiring. They lift me clean out of the post-Christmas trough of despond.

I am grateful for the lift the letters have given me season after season. But for some reason, maybe out of a yearning for a little variety, I keep hoping to get a Christmas letter that goes something like this:

"In re yours of December: We welcomed your Christmas greetings and news. As you might have heard, Mother and Father have separated and the children have scattered, so it took a while to pass your letter around, but all of us appreciated it. Truly we did.

"Our Ophelia is living with a nice young man in a commune in northern Orange County. He makes leather sandals and she handles the food stamps. They seem to be happy and that's what counts, we always say.

"Father Jim is out of work again and is talking about going into full retirement. He will be the first one in the community to do it at his age and without a pension.

"Our little Claiborne is flunking everything in school and the teachers keep complaining about his conduct. He dropped out of Little League baseball last summer and football this fall and has quit Boy Scouts.

"Our little Ernestine was doing real well on the piano until they came and took it away. We had to drop her lessons after they repossessed the car.

"Mother has gone back to work and seems happy enough, considering, except she says she can hardly stand being around pizzas all day.

"The horse ran off. The dog bit the insurance man and he is planning to sue, besides dropping the policy. The bills keep piling up, everybody has cut us off, and nobody knows where the next morsel is coming from.

"From our house to your house, best wishes for a holiday season abundant in spirit, joy and hope."

Keep those Christmas letters coming, folks.

12/28/75

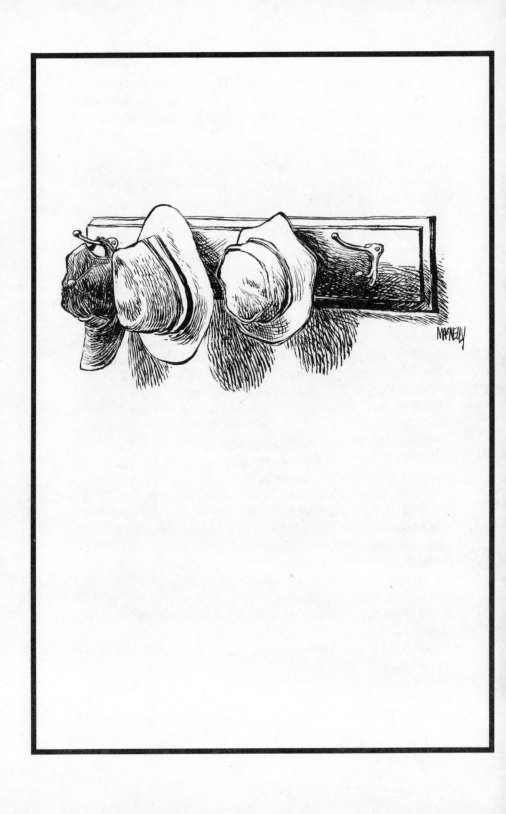

AFTERWORD

One of the occupational hazards for writers, even those who put one little word after another for reasons other than satisfying their basic needs, is falling deeply in love with their own prose. They dote on their work with roughly the same regard that a parent lavishes on a newborn child, unable to detect the slightest imperfection, in detail, in tone, or in full body. The slightest work can inspire a pride of authorship awesome to behold and to the author, if not to the casual reader, be a comfort and a joy.

One of the best newspaper writers was William Polk, who crafted editorials for the *Greensboro Daily News*. When he was on the brink of retirement, he talked in an interview about his life and times. The retirement interview, by the way, is the equivalent at many newspapers of the gold watch or the engraved plaque for placing on the mantel.

The interviewer asked Polk the standard question about his hobbies, what he liked most to do when he wasn't writing editorials or tending to duties at home. And in a burst of candor Polk said that more than anything else − more than golf or tennis or spectator sports or gardening or bird-watching − he liked to curl up in bed with a pint of liquor to sip and a sheaf of his old editorials to read and exult over.

I know the feeling.

Graybeards at the University in Chapel Hill get a similar warm and pleasant feeling going over their old lecture notes and scholarly publications and papers presented at the annual conventions of the Modern Language Association and the Association of Educators in Journalism and Mass Communications and other congregations of the learned. Most of the graybeards don't curl up in bed with a pint for lubrication, as Polk did. They like to stand at a lectern or a reasonable facsimile of one − maybe the butcher block table in the kitchen − to get the full force and effect of their eloquence.

I know that feeling, too.

My wife caught me at it in the kitchen one night, surprising me in mid-gale, while I was lecturing to a hanging plant, a spider fern that resembled in all but color one of today's coed hairdos. That happened to be merely a rehearsal for classroom duty, not a review of my collected lecture notes, but the warm pride of authorship was much the same.

I got an entirely different and altogether unwanted feeling in the making of this book, going through columns I had written over the last 16 years, about a thousand all told. Trying to be as candid as William Polk was, I have to say the experience was anything but warm and pleasant or a comfort and a joy.

In some cases, especially on the fourth or fifth reading, the experience was downright unnerving — alternately embarrassing, humiliating and mortifying. I wouldn't have thought it likely for anyone my age to blush, sitting there alone, with the door locked and the blinds down, going over something he had written 10 or 15 years ago. Given a choice now, I would chew up and swallow many of those columns rather than have them see print.

For an outstanding example, when everybody else in the country was writing about the terrible tragedy of Vietnam and how we were going to get out of that awful mess, I was carrying on at length about chicken feathers and manure and the pervasive smell of hogs in Chatham County.

When responsible columnists were examining Watergate and its implications for constitutional government, I was getting off one piece after another about sophomores baying at the moon at midnight in downtown Chapel Hill and bemoaning the loss of a diseased old elm on Battle Lane.

Then when others were assessing the Carter and Reagan administrations, I did a perceptive piece on trying to grow hair, and seminal columns on chopping stovewood and feeding heifers from a bucket fitted with rubber teats. There was also the ground-breaking piece I did on the heifers, once they became brave young bulls, tearing through the electric fence and mingling with Bruce Collins' purebred cows, to Bruce's everlasting dismay. I can't forget, although I have tried, the one about my pickup truck shuddering to a halt, sounding the death rattle, and dying in the middle of the driveway, blocking in the visiting preacher and his wife.

All those pieces have been excised from this collection, of course. Even so, the memory alone is harrowing.

Maybe if I had nipped at a pint, they way William Polk did, or maybe a magnum....

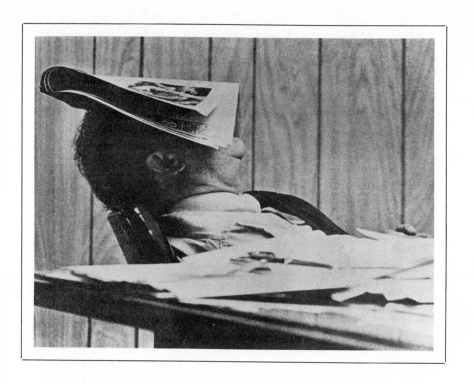